Warrior • 69

Darby's Rangers 1942–45

Mir Bahmanyar • Illustrated by Michael Welply

First published in Great Britain in 2003 by Osprey Publishing,
Midland House, West Way, Botley, Oxford OX2 0PH, UK
44-02 23rd St, Suite 219, Long Island City, NY 11101, USA
Email: info@ospreypublishing.com

© 2003 Osprey Publishing Ltd.

All rights reserved. Apart from any fair dealing for the purpose of private study, research, criticism or review, as permitted under the Copyright, Designs and Patents Act, 1988, no part of this publication may be reproduced, stored in a retrieval system, or transmitted in any form or by any means, electronic, electrical, chemical, mechanical, optical, photocopying, recording or otherwise, without the prior written permission of the copyright owner. Enquiries should be addressed to the Publishers.

Transferred to digital print on demand 2010

First published 2003
1st impression 2003

Printed and bound by Cadmus Communications, USA

A CIP catalog record for this book is available from the British Library

ISBN: 978 1 84176 627 0

Editorial by Tom Lowres
Design by Ken Vail Graphic Design, Cambridge, UK
Index by Alan Thatcher
Originated by The Electronic Page Company, Cwmbran, UK

Acknowledgments

Sara van Valkenburg. Angelo Munsel. Ranger-qualified Marine Sergeant Major James Dever.

Special thanks to Darby Rangers Jim Altieri, Carl Lehmann, Gino Mercuriali, Ted Fleser, Don Fredericks, and Phil "Snapdragon" Stern for opening up his World War II photograph archives.

Marcia Moen and Margo Heinen. Denis Muir of Achnacarry Castle.

Vietnam veteran Thomas Lanagan who transcribed his uncle's notes, Darby Ranger Thomas S. Sullivan, in meticulous detail.

Artist's note

Readers may care to note that the original paintings from which the color plates in this book were prepared are available for private sale. All reproduction copyright whatsoever is retained by the Publishers. All enquiries should be addressed to:

Michael Welply,
6 Avenue Nationale,
18340 Levet,
France

email: michael.welply@wanadoo.fr

The Publishers regret that they can enter into no correspondence upon this matter.

The Woodland Trust

Osprey Publishing is supporting the Woodland Trust, the UK's leading woodland conservation charity, by funding the dedication of trees.

www.ospreypublishing.com

FRONT COVER **Two Rangers representing the diversity of the men attracted to this elite unit. (Phil Stern)**

CONTENTS

INTRODUCTION	4
CHRONOLOGY	11
HONORS	13
ENLISTMENT	14
VOLUNTEERING	15
TRAINING AND PERSONALITIES	17
Darby and Dammer • Vaughan	
FATHER BASIL AND THE RANGERS	25
EQUIPMENT AND WEAPONS	29
ON CAMPAIGN	32
Food • Hygiene • The enemy	
EXPERIENCE OF BATTLE	42
Dieppe • Arzew and Sened, North Africa • Sened • 3rd and 4th Ranger Battalions	
Gela/Lecata, Italy • Mainland Italy • Cisterna • POW	
BIBLIOGRAPHY	60
COLOR PLATE COMMENTARY	60
INDEX	64

DARBY'S RANGERS 1942–45

INTRODUCTION

"Onward we stagger, and if the tanks come, may God help the tanks."
El Darbo

By 1942 after over two years of combat, the world had been transformed into a maelstrom of death and destruction. Wherever Allied forces were fighting, they were pushed back by their better-trained and better-led German and Japanese counterparts. Unprepared for the war it was entering, the US Army still needed to gain the confidence of the people back home. Positive action was also needed to restore the morale of the citizens of the remaining and ever-shrinking free world, while simultaneously providing hope for millions of the oppressed living in conquered territories. Britain's answer to the same problems that she had encountered just a few years earlier, was the creation of the Commandos as envisioned by Lt. Col. Dudley Clarke of the Imperial Staff and supported by Prime Minister Winston Churchill. World War II Ranger Carl Lehmann describes the Commandos as:

> ... highly trained volunteer "shock troopers" who could respond quickly to invasion or, as they did, carry the fight to enemy beaches with hit-and-run amphibious raids. The title, "Commando" came from that of the Boer guerrillas in the war of Churchill's youth. Commandos rekindled the belligerence of the desperate British

These Rangers best exemplify the naivete and innocence of men entering war. (Phil Stern)

Army after Dunkirk and gained the necessary experience for later, wider combat. Their raids drew increasing numbers of German divisions to the defense of the European coast.

In the US, President Roosevelt sought to create commando-style units to do just the same – strike back at the enemy and restore the confidence of the American public in the military. In the spring of 1942, Gen. George Marshall, Chief of Staff of the US Army, sent Col. Lucian K. Truscott Jr. to England to liaise with the British General Staff and coordinate training between the inexperienced US troops and the battle-proven British Commandos. On May 26, 1942, Colonel Truscott submitted proposals to Gen. Marshall for the creation of an American unit along the lines of the British Commandos. The War Department authorized Truscott and Maj. Gen. Russell P. Hartle, commander of all Army forces in Northern Ireland, to activate the US Army's 1st Ranger Battalion. The title, "RANGER," after the famous 18th-century Rangers of the French and Indian War, was selected by Gen. Truscott "because the name Commandos rightfully belonged to the British, and we sought a name more typically American." Initially and unbeknownst to most, the Ranger unit was formed for the specific purpose of training soldiers in commando skills and then reassigning them to other units, thus providing a well-trained and battle-hardened core for the new American units. On June 7, 1942, the 1st Ranger Battalion was formed and its camp established at Carrickfergus, Northern Ireland. The unit's core was to come from the 34th Infantry and 1st Armored divisions of V Corps, stationed in Northern Ireland.

On June 8, 1942, Gen. Hartle appointed his own aide-de-camp Capt. William Orlando Darby (a graduate of West Point in 1933) commander of the Rangers and promoted him to major. The 1st Ranger Battalion was officially activated on June 19, 1942. Maj. Darby performed exceedingly

Ranger Chieftain, William Orlando (El Darbo) Darby is visibly impressed by the successful ambush of a German vehicle by his much-beloved Rangers (1942). (Phil Stern)

well in organizing the unit within a few weeks after receiving his command. Thousands of applicants were interviewed by his hand-picked officers, and after a strenuous selection program of nearly two weeks at Carrickfergus, the 1st Ranger Battalion was ready to receive commando training at Achnacarry Castle, Scotland.

The original battalion consisted of a headquarters company of seven officers and 62 enlisted men, as well as six companies (A, B, C, D, E, F) of three officers and 59 enlisted men each. A Ranger battalion was significantly smaller than the traditional American infantry battalions, and the size of these companies was determined by the size of the small landing crafts used by the British commandos.

During commando training, on August 19, 1942, 50 Rangers were attached to a force of 1,000 Canadian/British for a large-scale raid on the French coastal town of Dieppe. Forty Rangers were attached to No. 3 Commando, six to No. 4 Commando and the re-maining four Rangers were attached to the Canadians. Ranger losses from these engagements included six killed, seven wounded and four captured. The casualties suffered by the Canadian/British troops were horrific. Dieppe taught the Rangers invaluable lessons which were applied to future operations. The importance of detailed intelligence and reconnaissance was fully realized by the Ranger staff, and Maj. Darby recognized the value of discipline and training. These were important qualities to help men manage and overcome the fear and subsequent paralysis inherent in battle. After

No. 4 Commandos and US Rangers disembark from Royal Navy launches, they are returning from a successful raid on Dieppe. No. 4 were the only unit to meet with success for the entire operation – as for the rest – all met with disaster. Lord Lovat can be seen with the still inflated life belt and stocking cap in the middle of this picture. (George Jones, C Troop No. 4 Commando & Harlan Glenn)

Dieppe, Rangers were permitted to wear the Ranger Scroll, designed by Ranger Anthony Rada, on the left shoulder.

Darby, now promoted to lieutenant-colonel, and his Rangers were given an important job during Operation Torch, the invasion of North Africa in October/November 1942. Attached to Gen. Terry Allen's 1st Division, they had to conduct difficult night-time amphibious landings to seize batteries that threatened the Arzew beachheads. Once they were eliminated, the 1st Infantry Division could land unimpeded and capture Oran, Algeria.

Darby and Terry Allen of the "Big Red One" (First Infantry Division) share a quiet moment. (Phil Stern)

En route to Arzew, the Rangers continuously reviewed their plans. Every platoon and section reviewed their missions. Plaster of Paris models, maps and intelligence reports were analyzed to find any flaws in their assault plans. The Dieppe raid was a vivid reminder that proper planning depended on timely intelligence and reconnaissance reports. There were two coastal batteries at Arzew, and the Rangers decided that a simultaneous attack was the best way to execute their mission. The Dammer Force, named after Darby's right-hand man Capt. Herman Dammer, consisted of Cos. A and B and seized the smaller gun battery at Fort de la Pointe. The rest of the Rangers, codenamed the "Darby Force," landed 4 miles northwest, infiltrated and attacked from the rear and secured the larger gun emplacements of Batterie du Nord. These operations were executed with few casualties on November 8, 1942, a tribute to the Rangers' meticulous planning and training.

After the successful attacks on Arzew, some Ranger companies assisted in mop-up operations of nearby towns. Training continued to keep the men sharp. They were attached to the 5th Infantry Training Center at Arzew to act as a demonstration unit for the newly founded amphibious-assault depot. January 1943 saw the formation of Company G which was to train 106 replacements for the Rangers. Company D, which had been reorganized temporarily as an 81mm mortar unit in Dundee, returned to its original function as an assault company.

On February 11, 1943, Cos. A, E and F, 1st Rangers set out to raid Italian positions at Station de Sened, Tunisia, which was defended by the Italian Centauro Division and the elite Bersaglieri mountain troops. With eight miles of rough terrain to cover, the Rangers carried only a canteen of water, a C ration and a shelter-half each. The raid was carefully planned and exceeded all expectations. After closely fought combat, it resulted in at least 50 Italian dead and 12 prisoners from the famed 10th Bersaglieri Regiment. Five officers and nine enlisted men were awarded the Silver Star for their part in the Sened raid.

ABOVE **Rangers review every single detail of the battle plan en route to Arzew, Algeria. (Phil Stern)**

RIGHT **Robert Lowell (then PFC, later a First Sergeant) riding; Sergeant John Ingram pushing. Lowell distinguished himself on several occasions in later battles. A dynamic personality in the outfit, he met his death in the bitter-fought engagements in Venafro. (Phil Stern)**

In March 1943 the 1st Ranger Battalion led Gen. Patton's drive to capture the heights of El Guettar with a 12 mile night march across mountainous terrain, with intent to surprise the enemy positions from the rear. By dawn the Rangers swooped down on the surprised Italians, cleared the El Guettar Pass, captured 200 prisoners, and then held their positions against a series of enemy counterattacks. For this action the Battalion won its first Presidential Citation, and Darby was awarded his first DSC (Distinguished Service Cross).

During the large German attack through the Kasserine Pass, the battalion fought a rear-guard action through Feriana to the Dernaia Pass, where the enemy was stopped. Afterwards, the battalion maintained outposts at Nogene El Fedge, and then moved to Gafsa and Nemours where it provided men for the 3rd and 4th Ranger Battalions, and helped train these new units.

After Tunisia, the 3rd and 4th Ranger Battalions, with the 1st Battalion as cadre, were activated and trained by Darby for the invasion of Sicily at Nemours, Algeria in April 1943. Maj. Herman Dammer assumed command of the 3rd, Maj. Roy Murray the 4th, and Darby remained CO of the 1st, although in effect was in command of what became known as the Darby Ranger Force. The three Ranger units spearheaded the 7th Army landing at Gela and Licata and played a key role in the Sicilian campaign that culminated in the capture of Messina.

The three battalions were the first 5th Army troops to land during the Italian Invasion near Salerno. They quickly seized the strategic heights on both sides of Chiunzi Pass and fought off eight German counterattacks, winning two Distinguished Unit Citations. Col. Darby commanded a force of over 10,000 troops, including elements of the 36th Division, several companies of the 82nd Airborne Division and artillery elements. Together with the British 10th Corps, the 5th Army launched the advance against Naples.

All three Ranger units later fought in the tough winter mountain campaigns near San Pietro, Venafro and Monte Cassino. After a short period of rest reorganizing and recruiting new volunteers, the three Ranger Battalions, reinforced with the 509th Parachute Battalion, the 83rd Chemical Warfare, 42nd Mortar Battalion and 36th Combat Engineers, were designated as the 6615 Ranger Force under the command of Darby who was finally promoted to colonel. This force spearheaded the surprise night landings at the port of Anzio, they captured two gun batteries, seized the city and struck out to enlarge the beachhead before dawn.

On the night of January 30, 1944, the 1st and 3rd

Rangers hold the high-ground during the crucial battle of El Guettar in Tunisia. Here Rangers helped Patton win a big victory. (Phil Stern)

battalions infiltrated 5 miles behind the German lines while the 4th Battalion fought to clear the road toward Cisterna, a key 5th Army objective. But preparing for a massive counterattack, the Germans had reinforced their lines the night before, and both the 1st and 3rd were surrounded and greatly outnumbered. The Rangers fought bravely, inflicting many casualties, but ammunition and time ran out, as all along the beachhead front supporting troops were unable to break through the strong German positions. The Rangers surrendered. Among the casualties were the 3rd Battalion's C.O., Maj. Alvah Miller, and the 1st Battalion's C.O., Maj. John Dobson, who was wounded. The complete loss of the 1st and 3rd Battalions and the decimation of the 4th Battalion ended the war for Darby's Rangers. Worn down by the continual fighting since 1942 and with an inadequate replacement system a number of "newer" rangers were transferred to the American-Canadian First Special Service Force. The older hands returned state side where the Ranger Battalions were deactivated. Nonetheless, it is important to note that the attack on Cisterna proved costly for the Axis as well as it helped blunt the planned German counter-offensive and thus thwarted Hitler's order to "Push the Allies into the sea."

No story of Darby's famous Rangers would be complete without mentioning the "Ranger Houdini Club." A number of Rangers who were captured during the battle of Cisterna, escaped and either returned to friendly lines or worked in conjunction with local guerrilla groups against Axis forces. The grit and determination of some of these Rangers demonstrates the type of people that were attracted to those elite commando units.

Colonel William Orlando Darby subsequently commanded the 179 Infantry Regiment of the Forty-fifth Infantry Division at Anzio. Later assignments included staff duties in the States, finally culminating with the Tenth Mountain Division in Italy in April 1945. Ranger Darby, age 34, was killed by a German artillery shell fragment on April 30, 1945. He was posthumously promoted to the rank of brigadier-general.

Practice makes perfect. Rangers practicing beach assaults in North Africa. (Phil Stern)

CHRONOLOGY

1942

January 26	The 34th Infantry arrived in Belfast, Northern Ireland – the first American ground combat forces to arrive on British soil in World War II.
May 16	1st Armored Division arrived in Northern Ireland.
June 1	Orders.
June 7	Formation.
June 11	The first group of 300 volunteers arrived from the 34th Division.
June 19	General Order 7 officially activated the 1st Ranger Battalion.
June 25	Brig. Leycock, G. O. C. Special Service Brigade, reviewed and inspected troops at Carrickfergus.
June 28	An advance party of two officers and seven enlisted men left Sunnyland Camp, Carrickfergus, Northern Ireland for Achnacarry, Scotland via Larne and Stranraer.
July 1	Rangers to Commando Depot, Achnacarry, Scotland to be trained by the British Commandos.
July 12	Pte. Lamont D. Hoctel, Company E, drowned during stream crossing exercise.
August 1	Battalion to Darlin House, Argyll, Scotland, for combined operations training by British Royal Navy
August 19	Six officers and 44 enlisted men participated in raid on Dieppe, France.
September 1	Battalion moved to Dundee, Scotland and trained with 1 Commando.
September 11	Pte. James R. Ruschkewicz, Company C was killed and Pte. Aaron M. Salkin, Company C severely injured in accidental explosion of land mine at Barry rifle range near Dundee.
September 24	Battalion moved by rail to Glasgow, Scotland. Assigned to II Army Corps and attached to 1st Infantry Division.
October 13	Battalion moved by rail to Courock, Scotland. Embarked aboard three ships for participation in Exercises Mosstrooper and Torch.
October 18–19	Exercise Mosstrooper.
October 21–25	Final preparation for Operation Torch.
October 26	Sailed from Clyde in convoy of 41 ships, excluding escort.
November 5	Put in at Gibraltar to tank up on oil and water.
November 8	Battalion landed at 0130 hrs in attack on French North Africa at Arzew.
November 8 – February 7	Battalion worked with 5th Army Invasion Training Center as demonstration and experimental troops.
November 9	Company C relieved of protection of Division Headquarters and attached to 18th CT. Assigned mission of blocking road south of St. Cloud to prevent exit of enemy troops. The company was badly shot up during this phase.
November 10	Battalion relieved of attachment to 1st Division and placed in II Army

Rangers during an engagement near El Guettar. Within a few short moments of taking this photo, Phil Stern was seriously wounded by artillery shells. (Phil Stern)

	Corps reserve. Lt. Col. Darby appointed town mayor. Battalion employed in guarding prisoners, gun positions, hospitals and providing security to town of Arzew.
1943	
January 31	100 men and six officers arrive from the US to form Company G.
February 7	Battalion moved by plane to Tebessa – assigned to II Corps.
February 9	Battalion moved by truck to Gafsa – mission given as harassing, raiding and reconnaissance.
February 11–14	Battalion raided Italian positions northwest of Sened Station.
February 15–March 1	Battalion utilized in reconnaissance and patrolling mission in support of the 1st Division at Feriana and Gafsa.
March 2–13	Rest and refitting at Le Kouif.
March 6	Gen. George S. Patton took command of Army II Corps.
March 16	Attacked Italian position in Djebel Ank Pass.
March 23–April 5	Patrol and reconnaissance missions at Djebel Berda, Gafsa, Medjene El Felg and Sidi Bou Zid.
April 10	Battalion assembled in bivouac at Gafsa.
April 17	Battalion moved by truck to Ouled Rahmoun.
April 18	Battalion entrained at Ouled Rahmoun for Nemours.
April 19	Authority granted to activate 3rd and 4th Ranger Battalions.
May 21	3rd Battalion organized near Nemours.
June 8	4th Battalion activated in Nemours, Algeria.
July 9–10	1st and 4th Battalions invaded Gela, Sicily.
July 9–10	3rd Battalion at Licata, follow-up operations on Hill 313 and Porto Empedocile.
July 21	4th Battalion Occupation of Salemi.
August 12–17	3rd Battalion at Popo di Norco, Monaforte to Messina.
September 1	Ranger Cannon Company is founded by members of the 1st Ranger Battalion under the command of Capt. Charles Shunstrom.
September 9	4th Battalion combat assault on mainland Italy at Capo Di Orso near Maiori, then cleared it and Minori.
September 9–23	Assault landing of 1st and 3rd Battalions to Maiori (north of Salerno)

LEFT **Ranger snipers cover Arzew sometime after the initial landing. Note Fairbairn-Sykes knife the Ranger on the right is carrying. (Phil Stern)**

	and capture/defense of Chiunzi Pass, Naples. 3rd Battalion to rest then German Winter Line.
September 11–27	4th Battalion cleared Sorrento-Meta and reinforced Salerno.
November 9–14	4th Battalion fighting around Ceppagno, defensive posture.
November 29– December 2	3rd Battalion engaged at San Pietro, Hill 950.

1944

January 22	Anzio: 1st, 3rd and 4th Battalions spearheaded invasion.
January 30	Cisterna: 1st, 3rd, and 4th Battalions launched attack.
January 31	4th Battalion attempted relief of 1st and 3rd battalions but is repulsed. 4th Battalion placed in reserve.
March 25	4th Battalion divided. New members assigned to 1st Special Service Force, while veterans sent home.
March 27	1st Battalion ordered stateside.
April 15	3rd Battalion survivors sent home.
August 15	3rd Battalion deactivated.
August 16	1st Battalion deactivated.
October 24	4th Battalion disbanded at Camp Butner, North Carolina.

The result of a successful Ranger ambush in North Africa. (Phil Stern)

HONORS

Campaigns

1st Ranger Battalion
Algeria
Tunisia
Sicily
Naples-Foggia
Rome-Arno
Anzio
Two Distinguished Unit Citations

3rd Ranger Battalion
Sicily
Naples-Foggia
Rome-Arno
Anzio
Distinguished Unit Citation

4th Ranger Battalion
Sicily
Naples-Foggia
Rome-Arno
Anzio
5th Army Commendation

Invasions
North Africa
Sicily
Salerno
Anzio

Raids
Dieppe
Sened Station

Major Battles
Arzew
Dernia Pass
El Guettar
Gela
Licata
Porto Empodocile
Butera
Messina
Chiunzi Pass
Venafro
San Pietro
Cisterna

ENLISTMENT

Young men have always been fascinated by the military and they enlist for many reasons. Certainly during the Depression era of the 1920s and '30s some signed up for the additional monies earned over weekend drills. Others may have joined the service out of patriotic sentiment. This was certainly true as America put herself on war footing against the encroaching Japanese menace and the reinvigorated German thrust into eastern Europe. Nonetheless, a large number of servicemen were drafted.

Thomas S. Sullivan graduated *cum laude* from St Michael's College in Vermont on June 2, 1941. A "slight, genial, intelligent, enthusiastic and much-liked and admired" man, Thomas loved to read and write. He may have enjoyed a distinguished writing career had he not been drafted into the US Army on September 5, 1941. He began his basic training at Camp Wheeler, Georgia within a week. Tom had an intense ambition to join the Air Corps as a navigator – after all, he had all the required mathematics and trigonometry skills. Sullivan also maintained a diary, contrary to orders, throughout his time in the military. While he was awaiting a decision on his putative aviation career he passed the time with guard and kitchen duties, reading, playing chess or cards and going to town whenever possible. His diary entry on January 4, 1942, however, expressed his frustration, "… still on Air Corps list. Damn the red tape."

He and his new friends would go to town and ogle, among other things, the opposite sex while awaiting new assignments. Chess became his favorite game as he thoroughly enjoyed the feints, attacks and defenses. Other times he'd watch movies like the *Maltese Falcon* with Humphrey Bogart. "It was an excellent mystery thriller. Sidney Greenstreet real good." Or *Citizen Kane* starring Orson Welles, which he thought to be "a strange story pregnant with hidden meaning. Photography brilliant – a new departure."

Weeks went by filled with various duties, while Sullivan continued to dream of the Air Corps, when finally on January 31, 1942 he noted: "We're packing for the North! Tomorrow a.m. I'll be headed for Jersey!!" Still hopeful of an aviation career, he joined the 34th Division at Fort Dix, New Jersey. His new unit was Company G, 168th Regiment and for the next few weeks more personnel arrived. Sullivan noted that with a few exceptions "all the rest can't drill worth a tinker's damn." It was clear he was unimpressed with his new outfit. Nonetheless, training continued. During this time Tom managed to meet his family on several occasions. He also attended mass regularly.

PFC Thomas S. Sullivan, "Sully." Last time home in February 1942 with his sister Audrey who gave him a diary for Christmas 1941. He was with HQ company, 168th Regiment, 34th Division. (Thomas Flanagan)

By February 12, 1942 Thomas Sullivan had come to terms with his fate – he was going abroad. His unit's convoy departed New York harbor on the 19th while Navy blimps hovered overhead. He noted "the Statue of Liberty is now out of sight. We are en-route." The convoy comprised ten destroyers, the *USS New York* and 20 transports. Various diary entries reveal the experiences of the millions of Yanks on their voyage to Europe. "Lifeboat drills, alerts and what have you. The food is fair, good, often terrible. Our quarters are jammed. We are sleeping in hammocks. We have daily Mass by Fr. Kane. The voyage is getting on our nerves. We have made a reading room of our cramped quarters. The air is sickening down here. We circle the decks. Officers have a beautiful dining salon – and we? The cockroaches are even on our tables."

By March 2, 1942 Sullivan's convoy reached Belfast, Northern Ireland. For the next several months continual guard duties kept the men busy. Settling in at their base, they enjoyed the company of the enthusiastic Irish. Fish and chips, movies, sight-seeing tours and learning the intricacies of Ireland's internal religious strife completed the education of the Yanks. Thomas continued reading books and considered the pocket editions to be "a great invention for a soldier."

In addition to the cultural acclimatization process, soldiers continued to train. Blistering road marches lasting seven hours and covering 22 miles provoked unpleasant thoughts in most men. And the unabating winds and rain made for a "beautiful lush mud." Sullivan was learning the skills of a radio operator. Then one day, in late May or early June, 1942, the news spread throughout the camp that a new outfit was looking for some tough volunteers: a Commando-type unit, which would take the fight to the Germans.

VOLUNTEERING

An official communiqué outlining the new unit stated on June 1, 1942:

> Since we are starting late in the organization of the unit which will be operating alongside similar British Units, with much experience, it is of the utmost importance that personnel selected for this unit be fully trained soldiers of the highest possible type.
>
> Officers and non-commissioned officers should possess qualities of leadership of a high order, with particular emphasis upon initiative, judgment and common sense. All officers and men should possess natural athletic ability, physical stamina, and should be without physical defects. While mental requirements demand only alertness and initiative, it is highly desirable that keen and intelligent personnel be selected; otherwise, much of the experience gained will not be utilized. No age limit is prescribed, but it is noteworthy that British Commandos average about twenty-five years of age.
>
> It is to be noted that Commando training involves a number of specialties in addition to physical training and qualification in arms. Among the specialties not listed in the table of organization are: Demolition Personnel, Mechanics, Truck and Tractor Drivers, Maintenance Personnel and the like. Special attention should be

given to selecting men with desired specialist qualifications; physical standards and a high degree of training in order to reduce to a minimum the necessary period of preliminary training.

In addition to the specialists indicated above, personnel with experience in the following are particularly desirable:

> Judo
> Scouts (men versed in woodcraft) – especially important
> Men experienced in small boats – especially important
> Mountaineers
> Seamen
> Engineers (Demolitions and Pioneers)
> Men with knowledge of railway engines
> Weapons specialists – especially important
> Men with some knowledge of power plants, radio stations, etc. to facilitate demolitions.

Hard-core. (Phil Stern)

Certainly, this was not an ordinary outfit. Men flocked to the call of adventure and mystique, or volunteered simply to get away from their current units.

Like 2,500 others, Thomas Sullivan knocked on the door of his C.O.'s (Commanding Officer) office whereupon he was asked a few questions about his desires and reasons for wanting to join the new unit. Once found suitable, he was placed on a list for medical examination and possible further questioning, this time by the men he intended to join. Why Thomas "Sully" Sullivan volunteered is really guesswork. He probably felt a desire to accomplish more and to meet a challenge. After all, his standards seemed to be high and the Rangers were a unique outfit. The Air Corps was out, but radio communications were beginning to be interesting. Nevertheless, he notified his chain of command and was forwarded for a battery of medical tests.

The following diary entries by Sully best describe the experiences of those tumultuous days:

> 6/8/42: Physical exam for Rangers – American commando organization to be formed at Carrickfergus. There will be ten days testing.
> 6/10/42: Radio code practice in Quonset Hut shelter. Am doing about 14 words. Don't know whether to join Rangers or not if it means giving up radio.
> 6/11/42: Called for interview before board of officers. Evidently accepted for Rangers. Yep, made first step. John Doss here too.
> 6/12/42: Joined 1st Ranger BN, American commandos for ten day trial. Unit composed of picked men. Wood, Hasting, Doss are here.
> 6/13/42: Speed march under Lt. Knudsen – damned blisters bothersome. Stationed in Carrickfergus near Belfast. Beautiful waterfront, medieval castle.
> 6/14/42: Speed – essence of commando training. Visit Belfast – 168th on maneuvers. Dick Porter joined up with Sextus.

6/15/42: Training Sundays. Camp cleaned up, boxed – will move.

6/16/42: 132 men sent back after interview. Companies of 60-plus men to be organized. Lt. Klefman looking for radioman. I have hopes.

6/17/42: Assigned A Company, Capt. Steve Meade commanding. Speed marches a.m., calisthenics, tumbling, jiu-jitsu and sports p.m. Day ends at 5.

6/20/42: Speed marches as always. Tumbling getting interesting. Fast volleyball game today. John Doss and I see *H.M. Pulhouse Esq.*, [starring Robert Young].

6/21/42: Expect to go to Scotland for training. No weekend passes. Doss and I chat with lighthouse keepers. John Paul Jones' shelled town was here. (A founder of the US Navy, 18th Century.)

6/24/42: Guard duty. To think I gave up HQ for this! All we have are the 536 radios now. Officers thrilled as if they were new toys.

6/26/42: Major Darby an impressive man – real soldier all the way, graduate of West Point, aide to Gen. Hartle.

6/27/42: Brigadier Leacock of Commandos gives talk on our training to be. Major Darby originator of Rangers addresses us.

6/28/42: Went to Confession at St. Michaels. Priest rather old, very interesting and amiable fellow.

6/29/42: New equipment in supply. Cleaning cosmoline from rifles – a messy job.

6/30/42: Confined to camp. Issued entire new outfit from O.D.s to rifle. All equipped with M-1s, Tommy guns, B.A.R.s.

7/1/42: Leave for Scotland via Lorries and Steamers. We train all night and pass through Glasgow and are in Highlands. Mountains all around us.

A Company Commander, First Ranger Battalion, Sullivan's CO. (Phil Stern)

TRAINING AND PERSONALITIES

Approximately 700 of the volunteers survived two weeks of testing and training. The rest were RTU'ed (returned to unit of origin). The survivors formed a battalion. On June 28 Darby's 1st Ranger Battalion moved to the Commando Training Depot at Achnacarry Castle, Scotland. The surplus 200 were RTU'ed at the Commando Depot. The First Ranger Battalion comprised 26 officers and 488 men ready for commando training.

Darby and Dammer

The two most influential American officers that molded the 1st Ranger Battalion into a sharp spearhead unit were the battalion commander, Maj. William Darby, and his executive officer, Capt. Herman Dammer. Darby Ranger Warren Evans who received a battlefield commission with the Rangers recalls:

Dammer was Darby's right hand man, a detail man. He did not have the flair that Darby had but was probably the better planner. With Dammer, everything was thought through carefully. Darby was a more emotional and inspirational-type leader ... After we had an action, Darby's after-battle-report would be very colorful. Dammer's report, on the other hand, was dry and to the point, very sterile. They were completely different men. Darby followed the book on how to be a good leader, although he was somewhat carelessly flamboyant at times. He was not demanding but we knew he meant what he said. We admired him even more because he was in on all the action with us.

Vaughan

At Achnacarry, Scotland the Americans were introduced to the man tasked with guiding the training of the Rangers – Lt. Col. Charles Vaughan, a ruddy-cheeked, husky British officer who radiated enthusiasm and goodwill. Darby recalls his impressions of the task master:

The tremendous personality of Colonel Vaughan pervaded the atmosphere of the Commando Depot. A former Guards drill sergeant and an officer in World War I with later experience in commando raids in World War II, he was highly qualified for his job. He had served with distinction during the commando raids against Vaagso and the Lofoten Islands in Norway. A burly man, about six feet two, strongly built and of ruddy complexion, he had a face which at times showed storm clouds and at other times, warm sunniness. A man of about 50 years of age, he was in excellent physical condition and was remarkably agile. He was constantly in the field, participating in, observing, and criticizing the training of the men. During it all he was highly enthusiastic. Observing a mistake he would jump in and personally demonstrate how to

The two most important personalities that shaped the first Ranger Battalion, Lt. Col Vaughan (left) and Major Darby (right). (Jim Altieri collection, ASC)

correct it. He insisted on rigid discipline, and officers and men alike respected him. He was quick to think up means of harassing the poor weary Rangers, and as he put it, "To give all members the full benefit of the course." The British Commandos did all in their power to test us to find out what sort of men we were. Then, apparently liking us, they did all in their power to prepare us for battle. There were British veterans who had raided Norway at Vaagso and at the Lofoten Islands, men who had escaped from Singapore, and others who had slipped from the Italians in Somaliland. As instructors at the depot, these men were a constant source of inspiration to my Rangers and, at the same time, a vivid reminder of the difficulties of the job ahead. At the beginning of the training, in the presence of the commanding officer of the Commando Depot, I told the Ranger officers that they would receive the same training as their men. Furthermore, the ranking officer present was to be the first to tackle every new obstacle, no matter what its difficulty. I included myself in this rule, believing deeply that no American soldier will refuse to go as far forward in combat as his officer.

This intense training course was instrumental in the Rangers' ability to close with the enemy and when necessary dispatch him hand-to-hand. (Jim Altieri collection, ASC)

Training for the Rangers was threefold. It included physical fitness, weapons familiarity and small unit tactics. Speed marches (at 5 miles an hour), log drills, borrowed from ancient Scottish games, and hand-to-hand combat were a main staple. Obstacle courses required stamina, shooting ability and finally, when completely exhausted, ferocious bayonet drills. The two-man buddy system was perfected. One Ranger would move forward while another would provide covering fire. Live fire exercises with "enemy rounds" striking around the Rangers provided realistic training. Innovative training equipment included bullets made of soap.
The Ranger Training Outline for all Companies listed the following:

General Subjects
I Physical conditioning
    A   Obstacle course 1-2-3
    B   Me & my PAL

C	M.G. assault course
D	Marches
E	Close order drill
F	Manual of arms

II Weapons Training
A	Rifle M-I-.03
B	Tommy gun
C	B.A.R.
D	Pistol
E	Mortar
F	L.M.G.
G	Rocket gun
H	Bayonet

III Marksmanship
A	Preliminary
B	Range firing
C	Target designation
D	Range estimation
E	Firing at combat distances

IV Care & Cleaning of Equipment
V Security
VI Tactics
A	Employment of weapons
B	Organization of defensive position
C	Terrain appreciation

This type of training was far superior to anything American men were taught during basic training. Sullivan was certainly impressed by his instructors and we join him upon arrival at Spean Bridge near Achnacarry:

> 7/2/42: Met by Highlanders band in kilts, bagpipes and all. March to Achnacarry, commando depot. We live in tents.
>
> 7/3/42: Sgt. Major McCaughan assigned as instructor to A Co. – an Irishman with 16 years in the Army. Five mile speed march – a pip (a black mark – failure to meet a standard) is dropped out. Two hours with packs.
>
> 7/4/42: Independence Day in British camp – they work pants off us. Sgt Major had American Marines here a week ago. Edstrom passes out after Japanese stranglehold.
>
> 7/5/42: We sleep on ground in shelter bags. During day, blankets folded, clean towel at top, with [barracks] bag in back, equipment on top – a neat but trying arrangement in cramped quarters.
>
> 7/6/42: Tents are teepee style. We are jammed with six. British had 23 around center pole!
>
> 7/7/42: Food wholesome but scarce, no seasoning. Tea, fish, porridge, prunes with cornstarch sauce seems to be chief diet. Mess officer has temerity to ask if we like it.
>
> 7/8/42: Reveille at 6:45, breakfast at 8:30, training 9 to 1, dinner at 2, supper at 7. Physical training instructors very good. Commandos rugged, real fellows. Unarmed combat.

7/9/42: Speed march over mountains. Saw large herd of deer in valley. Assault courses galore. Mountain climbing. Toggle-rope bridges across streams.

7/10/42: Use Tommy guns in "My Pal" assault course. Sgt. Major a marvelous shot with any weapon. Shoot .55 anti-tank rifle – Hell-of-a-kick . Accurate – pass excellent.

7/11/42: Fastest speed march yet –thought I was out on my feet but made it. Rope bridges, two ropes over river. I got almost across when palomp and an icy splash!

7/12/42: Scaled down – abseiling – castle sheer drop of forty feet. Most of us burn or blister hands and thighs. Captain [Meade] first as always.

7/13/42: Church services by Chaplain Markham of 34th Division from Ireland. Movies at night. I enjoy *Philadelphia Story* much more this time.

7/15/42: All day hike over three mountain ranges – cold, rainy on peak where we bivouac for dinner. Up and down hills, mountains, streams – return 8:15 at night.

7/16/42: PT with logs and lay in the ground muddy. No word at all of old outfit.

7/17/42: Swim rivers with packs – feels like Naragansett Bay in January. All I miss are the ice floes. Detachment arrives from the States.

7/18/42: Spirit and devil-may-care attitude of Americans amazes British and Scotch. Commandos go wild over Garand rifle [M1], we over Bren and anti-tank rifles.

7/19/42: Lt. Whitfield of the No. 1 Commandos is best liked of all officers – very tall, lithe – can out-walk any man I ever saw.

7/21/42: Don't know about Army, but British Commandos are real fighting men – London Police training , also Free French.

7/22/42: Hathaway, Wallsmith et moi are fifth columnists disguised as sheepherders we meet Mr Camerun and ten sheep inside Spean Bridge. Problem a success.

7/23/42: Old Mr Camerun's sheepdog was a marvel to behold – the way he handled those sheep. We got captured only because of GI shoes.

7/24/42: Fell out on speed march to Spean Bridge – ran a county mile – but couldn't catch up. Whitfield [1st LT, Commando] views with disgust. Tsk. Tsk.

7/25/42: Run opposed landing under heavy fire, live ammunition of course. A.P. [Associated Press] reporter impressed as Bren gunner splashes 303's about him.

7/26/42: 1st Sgt F. Co. shot in royal posterior – of all places. Rope bridge and death slide (40 feet down rope across river via toggle-rope) under fire for General.

7/29/42: Speed march about 12 miles around Loch Lochiel – bivouac for dinner- scouted by enemy – cross canal by rope – all night march and dawn attack across river on castle.

7/30/42: After 3 hour layover in cold and wet we force march thru' underbrush to Achnacarry and attack castle at 6 a.m. The river was swift and cold as Vermont winter.

Rangers toss a log back and forth as part of the rigid physical training program they undergo in Britain. July 1942. (Jim Altieri collection, ASC)

7/31/42: Layover – slept all day yesterday. Had few beers in canteen – still only one half-way pretty in there – Marie – then to bed.
8/1/42: Getting ready to move out. Free French marched out days ago.

Although completion of training at the Commando Depot afforded those Rangers the right to wear the British Commando green beret and the tartan of the Clan Cameron of Lochiel, the US Army and Maj. Darby disallowed its usage.

The 1st Ranger Battalion moved to Argyll, Scotland on August 1 for amphibious training with the Royal Navy. Shortly after the raid on Dieppe, the battalion moved to Dundee for coastal raiding training. The Rangers practiced attacking pillboxes, gun batteries, and other coastal defenses. In Dundee, the Rangers stayed with families in town as there were no barracks available to them. To this date, there is a close relationship between the Rangers and their host families. The Rangers left Dundee for Glasgow on September 24th, 1942 and were attached to the 1st Infantry Division. At Corker Hill, fresh from advanced training in the Highlands and Dundee, the Rangers were ordered to embark for parts unknown.

US Rangers training in the British Isles, swim a stream with full equipment. July 1942. (Jim Altieri collection, ASC)

Each squad was living in a pyramidal tent along company "streets" awash in soupy mud. They continued training until the end of October when they boarded the *Ulster Monarch, Royal Scotsman,* and the *Royal Ulsterman,* bound for North Africa.

Sully notes the harsh training as well as off-duty activities. Of great interest is the housing arrangement for the Rangers:

> 8/2/42: Arrive Rushven – most desolate spot on point of land off Hebrides for amphibious training and weapons training. Ten to 14 days.
>
> 8/3/42: Got boats and leather jerkins today. Sure need boats here. What a pip of an obstacle course here – up cliffs 12 feet, jump, log climbing, rope ladders, etc.
>
> 8/4/42: In "R" boats (small crafts) – beautiful spot, wild, rugged.
>
> 8/5/42: Desolate – five mile walk over mountain to civilization and by boat elsewhere. Firth can't be navigated at low tide. Practice landings tomorrow.
>
> 8/6/42: We crammed into our ride of R boat. Land dry on rocky beach – then wet landing – then another. That's all for today.
>
> 8/20/42: Arrive in Oban about noon. All ready for grand spree. Nice little town. Starks and I together – room in small hotel. Celebrate all over town.
>
> 8/21/42: We decide to stay another day, watch steamer pull out at 1:30. Bought some novels and maps, stationary. Sent cable home yesterday. Change to Temperance hotel! Having swell time.
>
> 9/2/42: Rangers arrive in Dundee – populace mighty curious of strange troops – sleep in courthouse tonight. We are to live in civilian billets!
>
> 9/3/42: Our house is with Misses McClaren, 39 N. Court St. – younger sister about 50 – haughty, domineering – other about 60, rather deaf, likeable. Well-furnished modern apartments.
>
> 9/4/42: A Co. meets in Baxter Park, our new assembly point. Whole city cheers us and gapes from windows as we march down flagstone streets. Large, busy town.
>
> 9/5/42: We ride to Mayfield parade ground each a.m. on tram – rifles, packs and all. Rangers are hanging from rear platform and everywhere. March past large beautifully hidden airfield.
>
> 9/6/42: Plenty of good restaurants, theaters, and even a beauty of an ice rink. People bubbling over with friendship and enthusiasm over us. We get canteen cards for food and sweets.
>
> 9/7/42: Roy and I sleep in big wooden bed with spring mattress, have own bureau, fireplace and commode. Miss McClaren cleans up room everyday, washes clothing, straightens up all.
>
> 9/8/42: Have had two dates with cute good looking brunette – Sarah Rice, about 19 – she does welding – all of them despise the English.
>
> 9/10/42: Speed march on hard road again past airport. Spitfires zoom out of nowhere and disappear as well into cultivated fields. Every inch of earth is furrowed. Wheat all over.
>
> 9/11/42: Saw Rangers in newsreels – A Co. under fire in assault landing. Enjoyed *How Green was my Valley* very much. Green's Playhouse Café is popular eating place.

The "Death Slide": Ranger zooms down the rope over river as machine gun bullets "tickle his tummy" and dynamite charges explode beneath. If he becomes unnerved and drops into the water in transit, he goes back to his old outfit. July 1942. (Jim Altieri collection, ASC)

9/12/42: Coca Cola at Café Val D'or – swell restaurant.

10/13/42: Went to Mass (served) and communion. Fr. Basil of Commandos said Mass in tent. Something big is coming off and Rangers will be in middle.

10/14/42: Rangers board train to Gourock and arrive on the *Royal Scotsman*. A & B Cos. with some Marines and QM [Quartermaster] are attached to this ship.

10/15/42: Gigantic convoy forming. Three plane carriers, *Queen Elizabeth*, destroyers and troop ships as far as the eye can see.

10/16/42: Practice landing from L.C.A.s [Landing Craft Assault] on concrete pier. Getting real proficient. Harbor crammed with transports, etc. – Dutch, English, American.

10/17/42: Sailing north to practice combined operations landings. 18th Infantry to land nearby. A Co. has toughest assignment – C, D, E, F to take out gun emplacements after mortars.

10/18/42: Landing by night. A Co. takes out simulated gun positions. B Co. forms defensive perimeter for us.

10/19/42: Quite a bit of confusion in the darkness. Cold, wet night on guard over bridge. 18th Infantry baffled upon meeting US Marines. Return to boat in L.C.T.s [Landing Craft Tank].

10/21/42: A.M. – heading out of Greenock for the open sea. Whither bound?

Course around Ireland today. Rumors flying thick as barrage-tallow.

11/6/42: At Gibraltar.

11/7/42: Gigantic convoy – five lanes of transports and two of warships on flanks as far as eye can see. A magnificent sight. 11:30 on deck in full battle dress ready to land.

The Rangers who completed commando training represented all types of Americans. The youngest was 17 and the oldest 35, with an average age of 25. Sixty percent of the Rangers came from the 34th Division, 30 percent from the 1st Armored Division, and the remaining 10 percent were from medical, quartermaster, and signal troops of V Corps. The Ranger officers did not field one regular Army officer with the notable exception of West Pointer William Darby. All were guardsmen or reservists. Although the enlisted personnel had come from regular army units, the majority of them were draftees who had volunteered for the new Ranger unit.

Darby's Rangers had undergone intense training for many months, ranging from basic infantry skills to advanced amphibious assaults. Men were killed during realistic training and in raids. The Rangers had become a hardened, well-trained, well-led and close-knit unit. They were highly skilled American infantrymen able to operate in any kind of warfare. Company D was also temporarily reorganized as an 81mm mortar unit but would subsequently be reallocated to its original task when the 83rd Chemical Mortars began supporting Ranger operations during later campaigns.

Rangers at Corker Hill, Scotland. Preparing to embark on Operation Torch, the invasion of North Africa, 1942. (Phil Stern)

FATHER BASIL AND THE RANGERS

It was also during the time in Glasgow that one of the most beloved and colorful characters joined the Rangers. Father Albert E. Basil, a chaplain captain, who was attached to the British Special Service Brigade, first met the Rangers when he arrived to conduct the funeral of a Ranger killed during a training exercise. Darby Ranger Carl Lehmann writes eloquently about the tremendous popularity of the Commando Priest:

During the drench of a Glasgow Fall long ago, a slender British Army captain appeared at the flap of Headquarters tent, 1st Ranger Battalion. His erect figure in battledress, topped with the Green Beret was militarily correct except for a cleric's collar and the effects of relentless rain. Muck of the company street compelled him to roll his trousers to mid-thigh and carry boots and gaiters. Clydesdale mud sheathed his legs to the knee.

With a toothy grin – mischievous eyes dancing behind enormous horn-rims, he announced he'd come to "look after" the Rangers. His lilting, melodious tones filled the tent and stilled tongue and typewriter; it slowed traffic slogging by in the Company street. It was the voice of a Burton or a Booth, whose whispers reached the last row. Cheery small talk and wisecrack in faultless diction and sculpted phrase stamped him master of the Tongue, honed as at Eton and Oxford. He charmed lately bored clerks and surly NCOs [non-commissioned officers], quickly learning their names and origins and regaling them with jolly quip and query. He was Captain "Father" Albert Basil, Catholic chaplain to the British Commandos, on ever-changing "circuit," "looking after" Commandos – now Rangers – whenever and wherever their units encamped.

One of the most beloved members of the Rangers, Father Basil is an inductee in the prestigious Ranger Hall of Fame at Fort Benning, GA. (Phil Stern)

Father Basil had first visited the Rangers when they were at Dundee for the final phase of their training before they came to the port of embarkation at Corker Hill. At Dundee he so impressed Col. Darby that he implored Brig. Laycock to allow the Father to come with the Rangers on the forthcoming invasion of North Africa. Basil was delighted with the assignment because he "had struck gold" – he was "looking after" a unit that was near 80 percent Roman Catholic! Commandos averaged, at most, two percent Catholic. He nevertheless looked after the Jew and Protestant, the same as he did the Catholic.

At Arbroath, a coastal town near Dundee, the Rangers concluded a training session and were dismissed to return individually to their billets in Dundee. The harbor area that was the site of their exercise was, like all potential landing areas, mined and wired as defense against German invasion. One man, jumping from a platform over a section of concertina wire, landed on an antitank mine that blew him to pieces and nearly killed the soldier following him, who was himself blinded and horribly wounded. Father Basil was in the operating room as a team of surgeons labored to save the man's life. One, despairing, suggested that in the unlikely event they were successful in saving his life, that life would not be worth living, and that he would benefit were he to die in that room. The suggestion gained some apparent approval among others. At this point, Father Basil said: "If that boy dies, I shall repeat your words to the proper authority." That Jewish boy still lives in Baltimore, Maryland.

According to Darby, shortly before landing at Arzew, North Africa, Fr. Basil came to him genuinely distressed because of his exclusion from the assault landing. He persuaded Darby to let him land with Battalion Headquarters. A few days later he said Mass over the first dead Ranger to die in Africa.

He had become so much "one of the guys" that many Catholic Rangers could not regard him as they did other priests and were reluctant to face him in Confessional. He understood, and engaged a French priest in Arzew to hear the confessions of the reluctant penitents. Since the Frenchman spoke no English, Fr. Basil furnished him with a list of sins in French with their translations, about which the confessor inquired by running his finger down the list, pausing at each item for replies from the sinner. When he drew a "*oui*" or a nod, he'd follow with, "How men' times?" Some young Rangers reported sins on that list they never dreamed existed.

After the campaign and more training in Algeria, the 1st Ranger Battalion was flown to the Tunisian front near Tebessa and Gafsa where it operated on the left of 2nd Corps, luckily free of the brunt of Rommel's smash at nearby Kasserine. Shortly, the Rangers advanced on El Guettar, occupied former Italian positions nearby and actively patrolled the desert wastes and barren foothills of the Atlas mountains. An outflanking left hook through nearly impassable mountain terrain brought the battalion down upon a superior, but shocked and surprised, Italian force. Father Basil, speaking fluent Italian, helped to induce the surrender of hundreds of Italian soldiers and earned the Silver Star for his part in that action.

Shortly before this, Gen. Patton, who assumed command of 2nd Corps upon Gen. Fredendall's relief, established an advanced headquarters in El Guettar. He lashed about with a will, yelling at any soldier without a tie or with an unfastened helmet strap. From his second floor office, he spotted Father Basil, dressed G.I. from head to toe, except for the green beret. "Bring that officer to me at once, I'll kick his ass!" "No you don't," said Darby, "that's our British chaplain, and you have no right to discipline him."

Sometime during this phase of the African war, the British Army located its chaplain, who should have returned to Britain immediately

A moment of reflection for these Vichy French soldiers. (Phil Stern)

after the landing, and sent for him. He ignored these orders at first, despite the threat to stop his pay. "I'll live off the collection plate," he said. Finally, under threat of courts-martial, he took tearful leave of his beloved Rangers. With him went a final collection out of a hat passed throughout the battalion. It was enough for him to buy a beaten silver chalice and have "1st Ranger Battalion" inscribed on its base. For nearly 50 years, as he daily raised it at the sacrifice of the Mass, he was reminded of the Americans he had "looked after."

Every man of the Ranger Battalion knew that rough language and bawdy stories did not disturb the Father. He'd heard all and still laughed at the dirty jokes and bawdy remarks. However, a blasphemy from which he cringed, spiritually, mentally and physically, was the usage of the Lord's name in vain. Soon every person who let slip a "JC" or a "Cee-rist" got immediate dirty looks from everyone within earshot. Neighboring 1st Division people were utterly confused by the Rangers' insistence upon the cleansing of their language when they were in the Rangers' area.

Many years later the padre revealed another substantial reason he valued his relationship with the Rangers so highly:

"When I first came to you," he confessed, long after the war: I'd had some problems with the Faith. I doubted things about which there

The first Rangers to die are buried in Arzew not far from the scene of the battle. The priest seen from behind on the left is Father Basil. (Phil Stern)

should have been no doubt; I was losing my focus during my daily prayers and wondering if I'd chosen the wrong profession. But then I was invited to an Ameddican [American] officers' mess and there introduced to your Ameddican Burrrrban! [American Bourbon] Suddenly it became clear what Paradise was all about! What nectar, what ambrosia! When I go to my final reward, I shall be seated at the right hand of the Lord in a mist of Kentucky Burrrban!

Apart from one brief visit when the Rangers were refitting in Naples, his duties carried him to other theaters of the war, and he was unable to look after his Rangers except through letters. He served with the Commandos in Greece and Yugoslavia and spent a considerable amount of time in the same commando unit as the author, Evelyn Waugh, whom he reckoned as one of the bravest of Commando officers.

EQUIPMENT AND WEAPONS

These four weapons were considered the main staple of a Ranger infantryman:
Automatic pistol, .45-cal M1911A1, 7-round magazine, weighs 2.5 lb (1.1 kg).
Magazine rifle, .30-cal M1903 and M1903A1, weight 9 lb (4.1 kg), 1905-pattern bayonet, 5 round-magazine.
Rifle, .30-cal, M1, US infantry basic weapon, semi-automatic, gas operated. Effective range 500 yard maximum range 3,000 yard. Cyclic rate of 20 rounds per minute.
Sub-machine gun, .45-cal M1 and M1A1 Thompson (or Tommy) gun. Weight 10.5 lb (4.74 kg). Modified version in 1942 had 20 or 30 round magazine with no front grip.

One of the specialty grenades used by the Rangers was the British No. 74 "Sticky" grenade. Carl Lehmann's interesting story depicts the ferocity of the Ranger spirit:

Although this Ranger seemingly is enjoying his food rations (C & K rations), note his weapon is close by, just in case. (Phil Stern)

Immediately after the withdrawal from Gafsa, Darby gathered his 1st Rangers about him to brief them about the next mission and to discuss the object he held in his right hand; it resembled a green duckpin ball with a black handle. It was the "sticky grenade" we'd used training in the UK. Though time dims some, most of Darby's phrases remain clear: "Breathes there a man here with soul so dead, who knows not you must pull two pins to prime this British wonder-weapon; the first drops the shell from a blob of plastic explosive, the second primes it with a 5-second delay upon release, which you do after you plunk it on a tank. Now, we're going to move in extended order across this plain; Rommel's tanks are running hog-wild and fancy-free all over. [Onward we stagger] should we see any tanks, God help the tanks."

When Thomas Sullivan was inducted into the army, he and millions like him received a basic issue of clothing and equipment. Additionally, Rangers received supplementary equipment and the second list provides a glimpse of that.

Basic issue Ranger gear

1. In this building you will be issued clothing and equipment, FOR WHICH YOU ARE FINANCIALLY RESPONSIBLE, in case of loss or damage. The items are listed below, in the order of their issue. Item marked with a double asterisk (**) will be issued you in your company. Items marked with one asterisk (*) are issued you upon your arrival in camp.		
Tags, Identification	**ea 2	
Hat, Herringbone Twill	ea 1	
Raincoat	*ea 1	
Liner, Helmet w/ Neckband	ea 1	
Shaving brush	*ea 1	
Headband	ea 1	
Tooth brush	*ea 1	
Cap, Garrison, O.D.	ea 1	
Comb	*ea 1	
Caps, Garrison, Khaki	ea 2	
Razor w/5 blades	*ea 1	
Cap, Wool, Knit	ea 1	
Towels, huck	*ea 2	
Meat Can	ea 1	
Towel, bath	*ea 1	
Knife	ea 1	
Barrack bags	*ea 2	
Fork	ea 1	
Drawers, Cotton	ea 5	
Spoon	ea 1	
Undershirts, Cotton	ea 5	
Handkerchiefs, Cotton	ea 4	
Shirts, Wool, O.D.	ea 2	
Tape for Ind. Tags, Cotton	ea 1	
Shirts, Cotton, Khaki	ea 2	
Canteen	ea 1	
Jacket, Field	ea 1	
Cover, Canteen	ea 1	
Trousers, Wool, O.D.	pr 2	
Cup, Canteen	ea 1	
Trousers, Cotton, Khaki	pr 2	
Manual, Basic Field	ea 1	
Pr. Leggins	pr 1	
Neckties, Mohair	ea 2	
Pr. Gloves, Wool.	pr 1	
Pr. Socks, Wool, Light	pr 3	
Belt, Web, Waist	ea 1	
Pr. Socks, Cotton, Tan	pr 5	
Coat, Serge, O.D.	ea 1	
Pr. Shoes, Service	pr 2	
Overcoat, Wool O.D.	ea 1	
Jackets, Herringbone Twill	ea 2	
Trousers, Herringbone Twill	pr 2	

Specialized Ranger gear

IMPORTANT INSTRUCTIONS TO: ALL NEWLY INDUCTED MEN (1st RANGER BN)		
Individual Clothing		
Belt, leather, EM	ea 1	(add) per EM, exc Ranger Bn
Cap, garrison, khaki	ea 2	(add) per EM, exc Ranger Bn
Cap, winter	ea 1	(add) per O & EM, exc Ranger Bn
Coat, wool, serge	ea 1	(add) per EM, exc Ranger Bn
Gloves, leather, heavy	ea 2	(add) per O & EM, exc Ranger Bn

Jacket, field	ea 2	(add) per O & EM, exc Ranger Bn
Leggings, canvas, dismtd, 1938	pr 2	(add) per O & EM, exc Ranger Bn
Necktie, black, P1940	ea 2	per EM, exc in Tropics and exc EM, Ranger Bn
Necktie, cotton, mohair, OD # 5	ea 2	(add) per O & EM, exc Ranger Bn
Shirt, flannel, OD	ea 4	(add) per O & EM, exc Ranger Bn
Shoes, gymnasium	pr 1	(add) per O & EM, exc Ranger Bn
Shoes, low quarter	pr 1	(add) per EM, exc Ranger Bn
Shoes, service	pr 2	(add) per O & EM, exc Ranger Bn
Shoes, service, w/hobnails	pr 1	(add) per O & EM, exc Ranger Bn
Socks, light wool	pr 6	(add) per O & EM, exc Ranger Bn
Socks, heavy wool	pr 6	(add) per O & EM, exc Ranger Bn
Suit, one-piece, herringbone twill	ea 3	(add) per O & EM, exc Ranger Bn
Trousers, wool OD	ea 3	(add) per O & EM, exc Ranger Bn
Individual Equipment		
Knife, pocket, M2	ea 1	(add) per O & EM, exc Ranger Bn
Roll, bedding, water-proofed M1935	ea 1	per O, WO, & Nurse, exc Ranger Bn
Tent, shelter half	ea 1	per EM exc AC cbt crewman, ea 2 re O, Exc Rgr Bn.
British Equipment		
Boot, vibram	pr 1	per Indivi, Ranger Bn.
Gun, AT, cal. 55	ea 2	per Ranger Co. ea 6 per Ranger Bn.

This equipment will be procured under arrangements to be made with Brigadier Commanding Special Services Brigade.

Battalion Commander will submit recommendations relative to desirable changes in T/BA at the earliest practicable time.

** The following inadvertently deleted from:

Motor Transport Equipment		
Motorcycles, solo	ea 6	per Hq Co., Ranger Bn.
Truck, 1/4 ton, 4 x 4	ea 9	per Hq Co., Ranger Bn.
Car, station wagon	ea 1	per Hq Co., Ranger Bn.
Truck, 1 1/2 ton, 4 x 4 w/winch	ea 1	per Hq Co., Ranger Bn.

A moment of sheer luxury after months of heavy campaigning in North Africa. The tub was found locally. (Phil Stern)

ON CAMPAIGN

Food
Although Maj. Darby had "volunteered" some of the regular Army cooks to the Rangers prior to departing for North Africa, the main food source in the field was the C-ration and anything else to hand. Rangers were infamous for their inventive ways of resupplying themselves, to the point where a Ranger supply officer came dangerously close to receiving a court-martial.

The Field Ration C consisted of small cans of meat and vegetables. Ten types existed: (1) meat and beans, (2) meat and vegetable stew, (3) meat and spaghetti, (4) ham, eggs and potatoes, (5) meat and noodles, (6) meat and rice, (7) frankfurters and beans, (8) pork and beans, (9) ham and lima beans, (10) chicken and vegetable. Other items included jam, crackers, powdered drinks, sugar, cereal, etc.

When you have to go, you have to go. More often than not, Rangers would dig shallow holes or small trenches and cover them up after use. (Phil Stern)

Hygiene
Living off the land and campaigning for months on end was a Ranger's life. When stationed or resting near beaches, it was naturally easy to keep clean. Ranger Don Fredericks recalls one incident where they rode on the back of trucks to a local showering facility for a one-minute soaping and one-minute rinsing off period. Clean as a whistle they remounted their trucks only to arrive to their camps dirty again. But the shower was great. While on campaign Rangers often had to dig small holes or slit trenches and bury excrement. Ranger Gino Mercuriali actually dug a small hole on the beach during the invasion of Gela/Licata, urinated and buried it. Later on, he discovered that mines were still spread throughout portions of the beach. The Rangers did discover lovely ancient Roman baths in North Africa and used them as much as time permitted. It was an experience few would forget.

The enemy
Upon reflection, Ranger Evans gave this appraisal of enemy troops:

> General Rommel, a German commander leading the Afrika Korps, was probably one of the best field commanders to come out of WWII from either side. We saw a lot of his men. Up until

A typical US Ranger recruit in 1942 at Achnacarry, Scotland, the Commando Training Depot

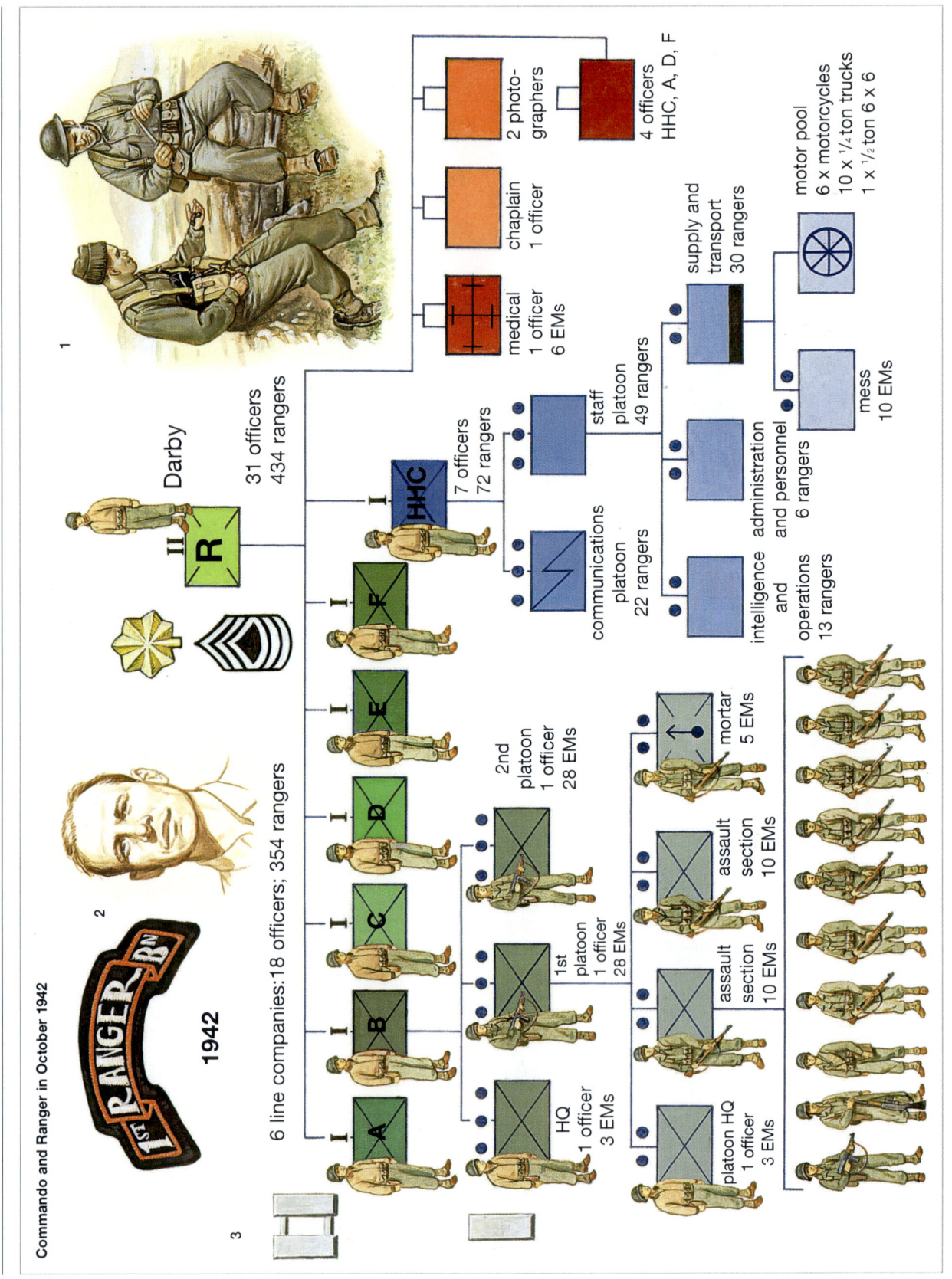

Commando and Ranger in October 1942

Raid on Station de Sened, North Africa, February 11–14, 1943, fighting Italian Bersaglieri

Darby destroying tank, Gela, July 10, 1943

Ranger, 1944

Ranger, Cisterna, January 29–30, 1944

Roman Coliseum PoWs

PoW escape

the Sened Station raid, we were no match for the Germans, man for man. I don't know if I should say that or not, but that's the truth. They were simply better than we were and were whipping the behinds of all the Allied troops. We hadn't been seasoned yet.

But as time went on, why, things changed. We became battle-wise troops and good adversaries for them. There were some crack Italian units that were good soldiers, but the Germans were all good soldiers. The SS were extremely good. One of the reasons I think they were so good, is that they were ruthless. Ruthlessness is something that can make a good soldier. And with Americans, many times, we couldn't get ruthless until we got really mad.

Not all the Italian civilians, or soldiers for that matter, were on the side of the Germans. In fact, we never knew which side they were on. I believe they were on the side of whoever was handy. I don't ever remember being helped by them, but occasionally we would scare one of them enough so that they would help us. We knew an Italian would tell the Germans where we were if he had a chance to leave. So, if we were behind the lines in the middle of enemy territory, and if we had a few Italians by our side, we'd keep them with us and threaten them with their lives. They knew what it meant when we pointed a gun at them. They were usually happy to stay. The Italians were lovers not fighters. That's all I can say.

I remember one time they gave up in drove about five times more of them than us, their captors. We just turned them over to someone else. The Italian prisoners didn't have to be watched as much as the German prisoners.

When bivouacked near the ocean, personal hygiene was easy. On the left is combat photographer, Phil Stern, on the far right is scroll designer, Anthony Rada. Cigarettes are the Rangers' constant companion. (Phil Stern)

Erwin Rommel is considered by many to have been one of the finest battlefield commanders of the World War II. (National Archives)

EXPERIENCE OF BATTLE

Dieppe

The raid on Dieppe in August of 1942 was the first test for the Rangers and provided invaluable experience for future Ranger operations. Although a number of Rangers never set foot on the beaches of Dieppe, the experience, though bitter and frustrating for some, was an excellent proving ground and further bonded the American and British commandos as well as their Canadian comrades. The official after-action report, written by Leonard F. Dirks, 1st Lt, 1st Ranger Bn, presents a vivid detail of that daring but ultimately tragic encounter:

> SUBJECT: Report on Ranger Detachment.
> TO: C.O. 1st Ranger Bn.
> 1. August 1, 1942, Lt. Leonard F. Dirks, six men from A Company, and six men from D Company, part of a detachment of Rangers under the command of Capt. Roy Murray, were attached to 3 Troop of 3 Commando. The group of 12 men were divided among the troop, three men assigned to each sub-section, the officer assigned to troop HQ. The troop was billeted together and the men from the Rangers stood all parades.
> 2. The training program consisted mainly of exercises over ground very similar to that which was to be covered in the actual raid. The first exercise was made during daylight hours on the Isle of Wight, those that followed took place at night. 3 Troop was the right flank on all exercises and had the 3rd Mortar section attached. The objective in all exercises was the same, that is the elimination of a battery of coastal and A.A. [anti-aircraft] guns. The troop for these exercises was broken down into boat-led groups, each boat with an officer or N.C.O. in charge of the men in the boat. The boat group was made up for L.C.P. boats (Landing Craft Personnel) and varied from 19 to 22 men. These groups were not changed except for minor details. There were five boats for 3 Troop and the mortar section. Several exercises were carried out without the use of boats over different ground but with the same objective in mind and the same principles involved. In these cases the men marched to the point designated as the beach in boat lead groups. These exercises usually terminated several hours after daylight and the troops returned to their billets, cleaned weapons and equipment and rested. Training during the time we were not on exercises consisted of weapons training, cliff scaling, fieldcraft and some range work. Cliff scaling was done with the aid of scaling ladders which are made of tubular metal, very light and about 6" wide. They are made up in sections about 5 feet long. These sections can be locked together to make a ladder of the necessary length. For using to enter buildings

A German soldier serving in North Africa during 1943. Note the desert boots. (Phil Stern)

or getting over walls, a hook can be locked on one end. A great deal of time was spent in swimming and a swimming class held for all non-swimmers every afternoon. Fieldcraft, including cover through buildings and streets, was conducted as a troop exercise, one section working against the other. Troop orders were posted on the bulletin board every morning giving the program and orders for the day. Before each exercise the troop C.O. had a conference with the officers and N.C.O.s and everything was covered in detail. Maps were studied and ammunition leads decided upon. 3 Troop's problems were complicated in that the 3" mortar section was attached, and one of the officers of 3 Troop was to command it. The ammunition lead for the 3" mortar consisted of 42 rounds of smoke and 72 rounds of H.E. [high explosive] for the two mortars. This meant that 3 Troop had to assist in getting 114 rounds of mortar shells ashore, in addition to their usual ammunition load. The disposal of 3 Troop ashore will show how this was taken care of.

3. Once 3 Troop landed, one section (platoon) made their way along the approach route immediately. Troop HQ, made up of the 3" mortar section, AT rifle, radio man, and sgt. major and runners, followed immediately. The remaining section was left to assist in bringing the mortar ammunition to the mortar site, dumping it there and then follow the leading section. The beach party with an N.C.O. with a Thompson sub-machine gun, a Bren gunner and a number two man, and one rifle man. This group was made up out of the second section and placed on the beach in a position to give covering fire for the 3" mortars and to give covering fire for the withdrawal. This was a last-minute change to utilize the L.M.G. [light machine guns] as they did not arrive until the day before the actual raid. The L.M.G. and the ammunition was handled by the three men. 2,000 rounds were carried on the boat. As soon as we landed these men were to unload all ammunition and to proceed to their position with 1,000 rounds, the third man coming back to bring up the balance of the ammunition. The troop assembled in a defensive position previously decided on, waiting for the assault, the assault to follow the mortar barrage. The time for the barrage was Zero plus 55 to Zero plus 63, the last three minutes being smoke. The assault for 3 Troop was made up of two waves, one section followed by troop HQ and the balance of two sections. 4 Troop was to land from the flak ship in L.C.P.s and make up the reserve. The withdrawal was set at Z plus 120, Zero being the time of landing. Except for the use of the L.M.G. everything was done in the exercises.

Royal Navy landing craft wait for last members of No. 4 Commando to return from attacking the battery. Smoke has been lain but is drifting with the change of wind direction. The gulley is the same that No. 4 had to scale through, cutting or covering barbwire to get to the top. (George Jones, C troop No. 4 Commando & Harlan Glenn)

4. The actual raid, however, turned out quite differently. Sunday, August 16, 3 Commando was confined to billets, except for necessary trips for supplies. Monday preparations began. Maps were brought down from Commando HQ and studied, ammunition and demolitions drawn, aerial photographs and a relief map, made of plaster-paris and colored, was studied. The officers and N.C.O.s went through the entire thing then the men were brought in and they studied the maps and photographs. Demolitions ops were distributed, the whole troop was then formed completely dressed ready to go, the troop C.O. then checked everybody. At 5:00 p.m. we boarded buses and trucks and went to the harbor. There we had about an hour's wait and then 3 Troop boarded its five L.C.P.s. At the last moment, I was placed in boat 17, boat 16 carrying troop HQ. I was the only Ranger in 17. We left the harbor and started towards our objective along with the rest of the fleet. We were to reach our beach on the left flank of the main landing party at 4:50 a.m.. Between 3:45 a.m. and 4:00 a.m. we contacted a group of enemy E boats numbers unknown, and were fired upon. We were at this time about ten miles from shore as I found out later. We were under fire from that time on. Our boat officer did not know his location because we had dispersed trying to duck the enemy fire. When we did get straighten around it was getting daylight, when we started ashore we were fired upon by coast guns and machine guns. We did not get ashore and I don't know what beach we were headed for when we started. Then we went to Dieppe proper. This was about 6:00 a.m. We were at Dieppe until 11:30 a.m. when we started back to England. Our boat broke down about 12:30 p.m. after some time we were picked up by an ML. At 9:45 p.m. we were back in England.

Ranger Alex Szima and a Commando light up after the Dieppe Raid. (Jim Altieri collection)

5. Ammunition leads – each man armed with a rifle carried 100 rounds and two 36 grenades and one 68 grenade. Rangers carried 80 rounds in their belts and two bandoleer and total of 176 rounds, in addition they had one bandoleer which was left on the boat for AA use on the return trip.

Demolitions – 20 lb of assorted charges were made up by the H. Q. demolition section. In addition to this four sections of bangalore torpedoes were carried. The ends of these torpedoes were plugged with plastic and detonators carried. The demolitions were split in ten groups, packed in US canvas field bags and distributed. Most of the demolitions were 10 (?) lb. Charges of plastic with tape to fasten them to the coast guns.

Dress – Commandos wore denim trousers with wool battle dress jackets. No leggings were worn. Rangers wore denim and no leggings. One problem with the Rangers was how to carry the grenades. This was solved by a number of men who took their meat can pouch off their pack and tied it to their belts. The canvas field bag worked very well for the demolition kits.

6. The conduct of the men was of the highest type, both under fire and in the normal course of training. A very friendly spirit exists between the men of 3 Commando and the Ranger Bn.

Arzew and Sened, North Africa

Sully's diary notes the first battalion-sized mission of the Rangers as part of Operation Torch and the subsequent preparation to raid Italian and German forces at Sened. The Rangers were tasked with a rather difficult night-time amphibious attack at the port of Arzew:

- 11/8/42: At 1:30 a.m., A Co. lands in L.C.A.s on dock inside harbor at Arzew taking fort in one hour. One Arab killed at entrance. C, D, E & F take F. du Nord with mortar fire preceding. Am guarding oil refinery.
- 11/9/42: Three snipers killed above us. Sniping all A.M. yesterday. B Co. loses one man. C and E called out to St. Cloud to reinforce 2nd Inf. Bn. We are in front now – night patrols.
- 11/10/42: No news of C Co. – reported surrounded by French. Lt. Klefman and Bud Nystrom killed – two swell fellows. C Co. loses three men – did beautiful job, capture 75s, back home.
- 11/11/42: Search Arab quarters for arms. Quite a store taken – plenty of antiques. Eight-hour battle with medics and MPs for snipers. No casualties.
- 11/12/42: Moved to school-house where 2nd Corps HQ are established. A Co. guarding HQ bridges and roads. Great to-do with truck drivers.
- 11/13/42: Still on C Rations – got 17 cases from trucks today. We stop them for speeding while a couple of us pilfer crates from the rear. Commandos at work.
- 2/9/43: All day off. Finished reading *Russians Don't Surrender* by Poliabior. Move by night 150 km to Gafsa, oasis on edge of Sahara. Camp in olive grove. On bitter-cold guard.
- 2/10/43: Dug in tent, floor lined with palm leaves. Col. out scouting enemy who is 12 miles away.

First Ranger Battalion on maneuvers. Many Rangers became so fed up with the constant training and other regular army duties, that they threatened to quit but only a few did. (Phil Stern)

Sened

The principal purpose of the raid at Sened was to instill fear into the hearts of the enemy. Capturing enemy personnel was a secondary task.

Bing Evans remembers his first experience in close-quarter battle:

One of the major battles of the Tunisian campaign was the Sened Station Raid. Now, there I was, just a brand spanking new 2nd lieutenant, commanding the 2nd Platoon of A Company and leading my men into battle. Sened Station was a German supply station for ammunitions and was kept heavily guarded.

They also had troops in there ready to move up to the front. It was important for the Allies to gain control of the station or at least put it out of operation. We were ready for our mission. We took trucks to a French outpost, got off the trucks and moved out cross-country, across the desert. So three companies of us, A, E, and F, led by Colonel Darby infiltrated through the enemy to about 12 miles behind their lines and got into the hills overlooking Sened Station. We were a group of about 180 men. From our position, we eyeballed the enemy all through the next day. We used field glasses to study their every move and scope out the surrounding terrain. We made our plan.

On the fourth day we patiently waited for just the right time to attack. The sun went down; the moon was not up yet. It was pitch black. The time had come to move out. We advanced three companies abreast. Not in single file or in columns, but abreast across the floor of that valley, A Company on the left, E Company in the middle and F Company on the far right. Instead of a long line going into battle, we had a long front. Each company had a different part to attack and a different objective. Since I was in A Company, I was on the extreme left flank and given the job of making certain that our group would not be surprised on that flank.

All of us wore black stocking caps. I don't remember blackening our faces; our faces were probably so dirty we didn't have to. I estimate we walked about three or four miles from our observation post to the Sened Station. We had been given orders not to return fire if we were fired upon. We didn't want to give away our position. We had enough experience to know that at night, if the enemy fired at us, they most likely were unable to see us and would be firing high. In any of our raids when we were discovered, it seems that was the case.

We advanced and got to within 100 to 150 yards when the enemy evidently sensed something and started firing. They probably thought we were a patrol and could scare us away. As predicted they fired over our heads. We just kept advancing forward.

The next thing we knew we were in amongst them engaged in hand-to-hand combat and very fierce fighting. But we had the advantage. With the complete surprise, we had created a real havoc. We were using Tommy guns, bayonets, knives and hand grenades. That's something that most infantry soldiers have never experienced, hand-to-hand combat. They usually never see the man they are about to kill. Very few of us did.

As an officer I carried a .45. I had it in my hand at all times. On this particular night, I had my knife in one hand and my .45 in the other and I was using both of them. We were fighting Germans along with some Italians. Then the sky became as bright as day. Our opponents began to throw up flares so they could see what was happening. At that point, they could see us and we could see them. All of a sudden, out of the dark came an enemy soldier. He was running towards me with a gun in his hand. He got very close. His eyes were big as saucers, frightened and wild. Looking into his eyes, I became paralyzed and found that I couldn't pull the trigger on

Thomas "Sully" Sullivan, Company A, 1st Ranger Battalion, North Africa, February 27, 1943, at Gafsa Oasis near the rail station, sporting a bar and a skullcap. (Thomas Flanagan)

my .45 piece. I couldn't do it! I knew he was ready to kill me, but I couldn't do it. Up until then I hadn't looked into the eyes of the one that I was about to kill. But now I did.

Little Tommy Sullivan, my runner, was probably five steps from me to my right and a little to the rear. Being my runner, he was to stay with me at all times unless I sent him on a mission. The runner is used as the main means of communication in case the walkie-talkies didn't work. A lot of times they didn't. Tommy sized up the situation and without hesitating, shot my attacker in the chest and killed him for me. If he hadn't I wouldn't be here today. Tommy Sullivan saved my life. I think Tommy wondered what in the world was wrong with me. I told him my gun jammed. But I think he knew better. I think he knew I froze on the trigger. That incident is imbedded in my mind. All of a sudden I looked into a man's eyes, a man about my age, and I was a softie. I couldn't pull the trigger. That's one of those times that I am not particularly proud of. I was not the hero, Tommy Sullivan was.

Sully, now a battle-hardened Ranger, shared his experiences with his younger brother Joe:

Dear Joe,

I was about to write you at school but realize you will be home long before this letter reaches you. You must have had a swell year judging from all reports. This past year certainly has been a wow for me. It will be a year tomorrow that I joined the Rangers. I was at Carrickfergus, Ireland there and crossed the Irish sea by the well known ferry from Larne to Stranraer in Scotland. The best time we had was in Dundee where we lived in civilian homes. We were at sea in a little Scotch riverboat for almost a month before landing at Arzew, Algeria. We had a nap there catching them asleep. Our first raid was at Sened in Tunisia, Feb 12 where the Rangers wiped out gun positions and massacred the outpost. That was quite an experience seeing the flash of big guns going off in your face and expecting every moment to go flying through space. On Mar 17 we got going again capturing El Guettar and knocking out Jebel Ank pass with a dawn attack on the 21st. We spent one night on top of a rocky mountain peak and were mighty happy to get off it. There's a lot more but that's enough to let you know we weren't having a picnic all these months.

I've been to quite a few cities, including Oran, Gafsa, Setif, Oujda, and Fleurceau. The best one was the summer resort at Montaganeur where English is taught in the schools. There are six story streamlined hotels there, big stores, and all kinds of native shops and fruit stalls. Perhaps you've seen the Roman pool in Gafsa in the papers. We swam there many times. The water stays at 70 degrees all the time. You'd laugh to hear one girl I met

Rangers who fought hard and trained hard also played hard. During leave, some Rangers enjoyed recreation within the local towns. This picture was taken outside a North African brothel. (Phil Stern)

trying to learn English – sounds like a kid in kindergarten or a five year old learning the first reader.

I hope to see Roy soon but it's pretty hard as I haven't even his address yet. Ben is somewhere in India bombing Japs I guess. The old gang is spread over the map.

The two cities I've most wanted to visit are still a dream. I've seen them both, too – Algiers and Tangier. One is all lit up at night like a big sprawling carnival at the water's edge. It's a free city like Danzig used to be. As you can see I've been transferred from the old outfit [3rd Ranger Battalion] If we are successful in this one, I'll be a happy man.

How I envy you all now. It is beautiful here but the beaches, dunes, cliffs and walks back home are even more so. I picked up a Dec, 1942 magazine yesterday and thought it was a long way in the future. Time stood still back in September 1941. I wonder how it will seem to be home again. It sure will be hard to settle down after all this bouncing about. It's a lot of fun in a way, but boy it can get boring.

Best of luck,
Tom

3rd and 4th Ranger Battalions

On May 21, 1943, in Nemours, Algeria, the 3rd Battalion was activated, followed, on June 8 1943, by the 4th Ranger Battalion. The 1st Ranger Battalion was split up, with A and B companies forming the 3rd Ranger Battalion, and C and D companies remaining as the 1st Battalion; E and F companies forming the core of the 4th Battalion. After a screening process and six weeks of grueling preparation reminiscent of the tough Commando training, the Ranger battalions were ready. The Rangers were small sized

Many months after this photo was taken in North Africa, two out of the three Ranger Battalions would be captured by the Germans at Cisterna, Italy. (Phil Stern)

units, and did not constitute a full-sized regiment, so they became known as the Ranger Force. Lt. Col. Darby, at this time still the 1st Battalion's commander, would subsequently receive a promotion to colonel.

Gela/Licata, Italy

As the war progressed and some of the original Rangers took on more responsibilities with their promotions, less time was available for Thomas Sullivan to write in his diary. In this letter dated August 27, 1943, written in Sicily he gives his brother an excellent account of landing at the beachheads during the amphibious assaults:

Dear Joe,
Am very glad to know you did so well at Sacred Heart. I still have pictures of you in band uniform. They are swell. The fellows were surprised I had a brother so tall.

Although I am making more money now I haven't been paid since May 1. What a life for a soldier. On this campaign I was clerk, corporal, supply sgt., rear guard and ice cream eater (when I can get it).

Follow-on troops disembarking from landing crafts in the early hours. (Phil Stern)

The girls here, especially in the city, are very good looking and remind me of home, as do the magnificent buildings I saw in one city. Some parts of it did not look so swell. Most cities are old and dirty – often like Arab villages. Some are very modern.

The mountains here are very tall, rugged and very numerous – and I have been on top of many at over a thousand meters (4,000 feet). One I could see was taller than any in our part of the States.

The Germans are very good soldiers and hard fighters and fight to the end. The Italians are not so hot. We had a snap getting in on July 10 – others weren't so lucky.

It's a prickly feeling you get on an invasion. We could see the big searchlights on shore and the sea was so rough I got very seasick – first time – we came in small assault boats. I was very tense and kept gripping my rifle. As we were about to land I was raring

The results of a successful Ranger ambush, this German scout paid the ultimate price. Catana, Sicily. (Phil Stern)

BELOW Afrika Korps prisoners of war. Note the bleached field cap. Rangers considered the Germans to be excellent soldiers. (Phil Stern)

BOTTOM The face of battle. This picture taken near Gela Beachhead in Sicily serves as a reminder of the price paid by the individual in war. (Phil Stern)

to go – about that time a wave dashed over and cooled me off. We jumped into the water and ran ashore. Firing started and from then on it was *c'est la guerre.*

Joe, you should see an American cruiser shell salvoes of four guns as she sailed along the coast. I saw six big guns she knocked out – French guns. And Focke-Wulfs and Messerschmitts on the docks – like the movies. Two of my buddies captured some Germans who were terribly mad – they thought we were Italians because how could we be behind enemy lines?

It might interest you to know my old regiment really mopped 'em up last May in Tunisia. Many of my old buddies are prisoners now because Rommel nearly licked us last Feb. Col. Darby, they say, gave the Rangers steeley barks and said "if the tanks come after you, God help the tanks."

Did Marie get the Ranger patches I sent home? I hope you saw our insignia. We have a campaign ribbon for Africa and several regiments thought much of us and we are allowed to wear the pins of a French and British outfit (when and if we get them).

I have ridden on ocean liners, ferry boats, river boats, assault craft, a raider, transport plane, rubber boats, donkey, truck, jeeps, people, and everything but a P38 and submarine.

This life is very hard and we walked so far and fast many outfits are unbelieving. War is not easy you know and Jerry put up a hard fight.

You should hear these British. They're swell fighters. If it has been very bloody and you ask how was it – they'll say – "It was a bit sticky for a while."

Well Joe, keep on the ball, and God willing, another summer will see us all together again.
Love,
Tom

Mainland Italy

By the time the Rangers reached mainland Italy, exhaustion and illness took over, with many of the old-timers affected by dysentery and malaria. Others were just exhausted by the relentless effort of fighting grueling battles in the mountains against well-entrenched Axis troops. Warren Evans best exemplifies that emotional and physical drain:

In Italy the dates become blurred. All of those days run into one another for me. So many of them were spent fighting from mountaintop to mountaintop. One battle after another.

Once again we were to lead the way for the next invasion. On the 7th of September we

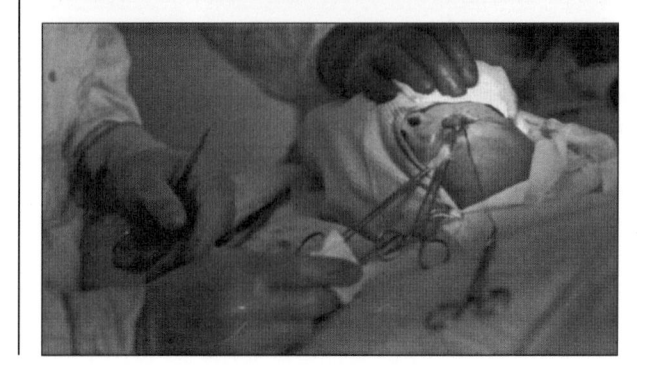

Battle-hardened Rangers during the campaign for Sicily in 1943. (Phil Stern)

traveled by American L.C.T.s and British Commando boats from Sicily and landed at Maiori, Italy, several miles to the west of Salerno. I remember when we landed on the Salerno beachhead I felt more apprehension than excitement. The excitement was always there, with each landing, but the feeling of apprehension was new. I felt we couldn't be lucky every time.

However, our landing was a complete surprise and we were very successful, once again. We went in five or six miles, almost straight up the mountain on a narrow road to Chiunzi Pass. We dug in on the ridges overlooking the Plain of Naples and the main road leading to southern Italy. But then we got into the middle of a hornet's nest and in the next ten days fought off one major counter attack after another. I don't remember the number, but there were a bunch of attacks. Water and ammunition were in short supply.

Our intense training was the only thing that kept us alive. Water was precious and brought up by fatigued mules, many collapsing half way to the top. To make matters worse, malaria contracted in Sicily was again returning to those who had only recently "recovered." [Many Rangers refused to leave their buddies at the front and would go absent without leave from rear areas or hospitals to join their friends.]

Because we took the Chiunzi Pass, we were able to direct artillery fire and naval gun-fire on the main highway connecting the area to southern Italy. We were probably responsible for the Salerno beachhead finally opening up. Otherwise, I have no doubt the Allies would have been driven back into the sea.

In one of those battles, little Tommy Sullivan was killed. That's the big problem of war, all of those people that I grew so close to and liked so much, well here I am and they're dead.

On September 16, 1943, Ranger Sergeant Thomas S. Sullivan, a "slight, genial, intelligent, enthusiastic and much-liked and admired" man, was killed in action by artillery at the age of 24.

Typical hill fortification just east of Ranger landings at Gela and Licata on southern coast of Sicily. (Thomas Flanagan)

Cisterna

Rangers once again led the way by spearheading the invasion of Anzio. Subsequent fighting to enlarge the beachhead by seizing the town of Cisterna ended in disaster when two of the three Ranger battalions were surrounded by German paratroopers and soldiers from the "Herman Göring" division. The 1st and 3rd battalions were all but wiped out, suffering 12 killed, 36 wounded and 767 captured.

Carl Lehmann was one of those Rangers caught in the encirclement that subsequently ended in his capture:

> The shell which killed Major Miller, according to what was told me by others near the time, was the one that opened the battle. Although I was unaware of the major's location forward of mine in the Pontano Ditch, the shell exploded quite near and with the explosion, I sprang running to the left, right through an enemy bivouac (no tents, just men lying under blankets), astonished at Germans rising all around, running away with hands in the air, crying "Kamarad!" as I ran through them, shooting from the hip. By the time I had expended the clip from my M1, I had run completely through the camp area, coming to a shallow hedgerow running generally parallel to the ditch, although now I was more than a couple of hundred yards from it. I continued my run up the hedgerow until my attention was caught by the clatter of a flak-wagon which pulled into view on a low ridge perhaps 100 yards to the left.
>
> Dawn was just breaking, and the flak-wagon was silhouetted against the lightening sky. I dropped, reloaded, and commenced firing at the soldiers who were trying to unlimber a brace of automatic guns in the open body of the truck. They were in plain sight and easy targets, and beat a hasty retreat to the far side of the ridge. It was then that I became aware that a line of Rangers had followed me up the ditch, many doing the same as I. (I had no squad at the time and was attached to Company H.Q., carrying a load of demolitions). We had quite a successful shoot for several minutes, at Germans whose heads we could see, but who see only our muzzle-flashes in the dark of the swale. All the metal of the M1 was hot and the wood was smoking.
>
> After some little time shooting one clip after another, I heard Sgt. Perry Bills shouting my name; after I replied he directed me to come in his direction (in an open field towards the ditch). I jumped up and ran to join those in the field, and the others in the hedgerow did the same, to the accompaniment of small arms fire, still

OPPOSITE Last known photograph of Sully, now with the 3rd Ranger Battalion, late August 1943, Messina, Italy. (Thomas Flanagan) inaccurate because of the dark. When I reached Bills' general area, I became aware of a large number of men flattened out in the field with no cover at all, and the small arms fire was building. I attempted to light a British phosphorous contact grenade, but it failed to detonate. A wounded officer nearby, seeing what I attempted, tossed me an American one with which I was successful in producing a cloud of smoke. However, I had had to toss it quite close to me because of the surrounding men, and perceiving the danger of falling tendrils over head, I again began running, not stopping until I ran into a fire fight between some 1st Battalion men and some Kraut infantry. I'm not sure how this ended but after it did, I commenced looking for C Company.

There was a tall barn nearby and I climbed to its second floor, which had a door looking south the way we had come, as well as another window higher up and facing west, which I attempted to gain for a better look with a handy ladder. No sooner had I started up the ladder when I heard the ungodly clatter of an armored vehicle outside. I abandoned the ladder and stole a peek through the door which revealed a self-propelled gun with a driver and a four-man crew in the back, working about the gun, directly under me. I dropped a grenade in it and hit the ground running on the other side of the barn before it exploded. I did not inspect the results.

As can be seen, I was running here and there like a scared rabbit, but I had a good excuse, I was looking for my company. I finally found Bills, a wounded Lt. Rip Reed, Scotty Munro, Larry Hurst, Hodel (the only ones I now remember for sure) and the remains of Bills' platoon, on the extreme right of the battlefield, and dug in with them there. We were about a hundred yards southeast of the farmhouse where I learned later Ehalt and his radio were. We could see distant scurrying German vehicles on the road to our right – out of rifle range, and all of the action was now going on to the north and west of us.

I was dozing from exhaustion in the early afternoon after the events at dawn and shortly thereafter. I settled with the remains of Bill's platoon taking an occasional shot, mostly long-range, at vehicles on the road. I woke to Bills' excited scream, "Them bastards is givin up!" By "them bastards" he meant our guys who were being marched towards our positions, bare-headed with their hands clasped over their heads. We

D-Day – 1 Anzio Beachhead. Capt George C. Nunnelly, Georgia Ranger, left, Capt. James Lavin, 4th Battalion Adjutant, and Lt. James Altieri, center, embark on ships (LCIs) destined to land them on the beaches of Anzio, January 22, 1944. (Altieri, newly comm US Army photo)

jumped to our feet as one and started running in the opposite direction – towards the beachhead. Not one of us tried to shoot through the prisoners.

We got at least a quarter-mile back towards the beachhead before we were pinned in a plowed field by machine gun and rifle fire from concealed positions. I was straddled with a burst and a bullet hit Larry Hurst. It was hopeless, and while somebody waved a white piece of paper (all our handkerchiefs were OD), we lifted our hands. Before doing so, I managed to bury a Luger which I had carried through Sicily and Italy, but forgot something else which damned near got me executed. The first German I saw was an officer in a leather coat running, pistol pointed at us, screaming, "Are there any more Americans out there?" Hodel answered inanely, "No capisce!"

Shortly thereafter we were marched into a farm yard and searched, during which I for a time believed I was about to reap my final reward. This little Kraut who searched me looked about 15 and he dearly wanted permission to shoot me because of "scalps" he found in my shirt pocket. The "scalps" were the Nazi wings worn on breasts of the tunics and coats of the Germans. During the time before we went on this last expedition, I had been the first in a hastily evacuated German position – a barn obviously used for sleeping, where numerous tunics and overcoats were scattered about. I stripped them all before anyone else came into the position. After separating me from the others, the little Kraut took this handful to the Feldwebel, begging him for permission to shoot me. The Feldwebel shook his head with a "Nein!" But the little bastard kept it up, drawing more headshakes and quiet "Neins." Before this played out, I was blessing the Feldwebel's obviously sainted mother for having birthed him. Before we were marched out of the farmyard to the rear areas, the Feldwebel came close and smiled at me, "You haff a Churman name, Carl!" That and what went before was worth the snappy salute I delivered and which he returned.

POW

Lehman's story continues with his time in captivity in eastern Germany:

Assembled with other Allied prisoners, after a few days, we were marched past the Colosseum in Rome for the benefit of propaganda cameras. It was one of the worst days of my life.

After short times in Northern Italy, and in Moosburg, near Munich, we were sent to Rummelsberg (Stalag II B). As we debarked from the boxcars (40 & 8s), we were informed that we

Time out for a coffee and a smoke: Corporal Pressley P. Stroud, Colonel Darby's personal field clerk, talking with British Commandos during a brief respite. Stroud was later killed by artillery fire near Cisterna, one of the smallest men in the outfit. (Jim Altieri collection)

This German tank destroyer was the victim of Ranger bazooka gunners, during the fighting at Cisterna. (Jim Altieri collection, ASC)

were to be deloused, and directed to put all our clothing on hangers for transport through a gas chamber to kill the fleas and lice, while we went into a communal shower. This detail is relevant (to me) because many years later, I watched movies of Jews put through a similar routine, with the identical understanding of purpose – fumigation of clothes and cleansing of bodies – except that, for the Jews, their shower-heads spewed Zyklon B. Stalag II B was a "work camp" where non-coms and others were assembled, and, if reasonably fit, sent to work parties, mostly on Pomeranian farms.

I joined a farm party of 22 American POWs at a place called Fairszien – a huge feudal estate complete with a mansion, extensive farm buildings, a dairy with hundreds of cattle, a schnapps factory and a group of residence buildings for the peasant workers. The prisoners were housed in a small two-story building; where the first floor contained a kitchen (also containing the bread oven for the whole estate), and two sleeping rooms for the prisoners. The building was surrounded by barbed wire. Two German Army guards occupied the second floor. One was fat, fairly jovial, middle-aged, and clearly unfit for front-line duty. The other was a blond, handsome Aryan with severe combat wounds and a very bad attitude. He had accompanied me on the train which transported us from Rummelsberg and displayed a particular dislike for me; this became evident from time to time during my service at that place. Other prisoners there were named John McMahon, Paul Sapsara, Hardenberg, Barnhill, Jackson, and Bill Space.

There was an opening in the cow barn and I took it, qualifying because of summer stints milking cows for Aunt Bea and Uncle Wilbur, near Betterton, MD. I milked about 30 Holsteins in the morning, 30 in the evening and a few at midday. The cows, confined to stalls, were fed little but chopped straw and some liquid from the

The Conca–Cisterna road in 1999. This area saw heavy action as the 4th Ranger Battalion desperately tried to punch through the German lines to help the surrounded 1st and 3rd Ranger Battalions. (Author's collection)

Disabled american Sherman tank and Ranger PFC Edward J. Hall, 4th Ranger Battalion, following the ill-fated attack at Cisterna. (Jim Altieri collection)

schnapps factory. Without pasture (it was March) they gave very little milk, so the "milking" amounted to "stripping." I was assigned an oxen (whom I promptly named Ferdinand), to clean the stalls and haul the offal (waste parts, especially of a butchered animal). The Kuhmeister ["cow master"], a German, oversaw operations, as well as the work of Barnhill, a farmer from Utah and nicknamed "Utah," and a Frenchman, Jacques called "Jock". The Kuhmeister had one of the most disagreeable duties of all, he had to grease his arm and reach in every Kuhrectum up to his shoulder and pull out that which usually emerged with absolutely no Kuheffort. A camp joke, shared with the Kuhmeister, was that he was grooming me for the "Kuhshitpull."

An open field en route to Cisterna in 1999. This is where the First and Third Rangers were trapped by the Germans. (Author's collection)

[After a thwarted escape attempt and return to the camp] I soon learned that there was a so-called Escape Committee – "so-called" because it never helped any escape. My application for its help was initially turned down, "because you don't speak German." I returned after learning that it had never helped anyone, and demanded its help on the ground that I indeed had a record of an escape, and if they were not going to serve me, then who would they serve. I also threatened to report them when the war was over. They reluctantly decided to "help." I was given identification papers as a paroled French POW, a document purporting to give me permission to travel to the next town, money, and a map and compass. I stuffed all this in my underwear and shoes and, soon after was assigned to a street work detail in a nearby town.

One clear memory remains of the work (mostly ditch-digging at the side of a street, for storm water pipe repair and replacement): prominent in the fill which we excavated were myriad broken black marble stones, such as are used for store fronts. One side of the slabs had Jewish characters scribed into the polished surface. Clearly, the "Final Solution" here as elsewhere, included eradication of Jewish characters on store fronts. This then added substance to reports of the horrors of Jewish persecution of which we'd read and heard of in newspapers and broadcasts back home. One of the fears we all had was for the Jews among us prisoners. Oddly, I know not of a single instance of mistreatment of Jewish POWs; actually, many were in superior positions because of their abilities to speak the language.

Another memory which endures is of the sometimes multiple "funeral" processions down the street where we worked. The procession invariably consisted of a horse-drawn hearse, a carriage for the elderly among the mourners, with most trailing, black-clad, behind. These were part of the ceremonies for Krauts killed on the Russian and Western Fronts; of course, there were no remains in the caskets, but all had a Kraut helmet riding atop them. The same caskets were used over and over. As the hearse went by, we all stood to attention, with bared heads and solemn faces, singing softly, muting the words, "The little black hearse goes riding by And you may be-ee the next to die." The mourners as they passed, smiled and nodded, "Danke. . . Danke. . .Danke" in appreciation of our "respect" for a fallen foe.

My exit from these premises was similar to that at Fairszien; weighing but about 130 lb, I squeezed through a narrow transom and between strands of barbed wire, then out into the streets. I had been issued a spanking new "Class-A" uniform by the Red Cross at Stalag II B which, with a red dye, turned the O.D. to an attractive reddish brown, and which, with a change of buttons and topped with a beret, made me one of the best-dressed Froggies in German captivity.

After one and a half night's traveling, mostly through woods, I got to the town with the railroad station where I was to entrain for Berlin and the "safe-house" nearby. I walked to the station in broad daylight, bathed in admiring glances from Frauleins unaccustomed to such finery on a Froggie or anyone else, for that matter. Unchallenged, I approached the ticket window, presented my "credentials" and requested a ticket. I immediately saw, from the expression on the face of the old man at the window and from his haste to get to the telephone, that a large stack of shit was about to hit the fan. I sprinted for the door, out of town and into a deep wood again where I kept going until nightfall. A change of plan was in order: the first one was resurrected and again – North and the Baltic beckoned.

After a few days though, skulking through the night country side, subsisting on raw potatoes and carrots dug from storage trenches in the fields, I became hopelessly sick with the malarial chills and fever again. I have no memory of how I got to a doctor's office and then back to Stalag II B and hospital again, but was told soldiers had found me at roadside. Again, after convalescence, I went before the Commandant and was sentenced to two weeks in the Cooler. He inquired as to my surprised expression and I answered that I expected more than three weeks, because that is what my sentence was the last time I escaped. He smiled and said, "It is a soldier's duty to escape –but don't do it again, *verstehen?*"

By this time, at about the end of 1944, the Russians were getting close and we were alerted to prepare to abandon the camp and be marched west with the population of II B, and the populations of its work camps in the area. The warehouse had a goodly amount of Red Cross parcels, and we were allowed to take as much as we could carry. We were put on the road, four abreast, with guards on either side from about January 1945, and marched west with Russian guns sounding in the distance. We kept on the road through January, February and about the middle of March, taking shelter at night in barns and abandoned shelters of many descriptions. A few escaped early and got through the Russian lines (one was Jack Fisher). Ruona, Kiernan, Johnson, Weakes and myself escaped from the column about mid-March.

Battle-hardened and extremely tough Ranger officer Chuck Shunstrum. Notorious for his aggression and battlefield leadership. A member of the Ranger Houdini club. (Phil Stern)

The escape occurred this way: uncharacteristically, the column halted half way through a day's march and we languished on the side of the road for an extended period. Then, we saw the head of the column, a half-mile ahead, doubling back – we were reversing direction! I said something to the effect, "Shit, I ain't gonna take one step back!" "Waddahya gonna do?", said Ruona, Johnson, etc., It did not take long: I proposed that when the "curl" of the column got to us, to run a few steps off the road to the right of column and flop in the knee-high vegetation. The guards on the left side would be unable to see through the column, and those on the right would have their backs to me. The other four immediately proposed to go with me, and we set about alerting the others in the column that we were leaving so's not to give us away. We were the last Americans in the column, behind us were about a hundred Serbs. The Serbs were great; when the "curl" reached us, we hit the brush after a few steps, and the column just walked away from us, with the Serbs stomping in step with their hob-nailed boots and looking straight ahead.

This image, from the corner of my eye with face pressed hard to dirt, remains bright as yesterday's. "Course, we were not quite free. I'd been out there before and brought back. However, this time we could hear Allied guns way off and the rest of the plan was simple; we'd march to the sound of the guns – not to the beat of drums, mind you. Actually, slink rather than march was the mode of travel, because there were many unfriendlies about. Much time was spent collecting food, since by this time we were completely out of the supplies we had originally. We dug through covered trenches in the fields, not knowing whether we would find the potato, carrot or, most likely, the hated rutabaga or sugar beet. Hated or not we ate them. In a barn, we loaded up with wheat, and learned, after much trial and error, there is no way to eat wheat, unless it is ground. Fortunately, in another barn we found a mill with which we ground our wheat by pulling the belt meant to be driven by an electric motor. A lowlight (heaven knows why such is so clearly remembered) of our scrounging was the discovery of a part packet of caraway seeds which we carefully separated into five equal piles, for flavoring our (unleavened) biscuits, i.e. cakes of flour, salt and water baked in the coals of a fire.

One day in April, we were deep in a forest, when we awoke to the sound of small arms fire. We decided to hunker down right there and let the war pass us by. However, late in the day there was a crashing through the forest by three soldiers hurrying along. To my amazement, they wore the green beret –they were a lieutenant, a sergeant and a private out of No. 1 Commando, the unit we had trained with in Scotland! I ran after them and after some hasty consultation, they decided to adopt our plan and wait for the lines to come over us. Their outfit had been in a fire fight the night before and they were separated and quite lost at the time we found them. During the two days we laid low in that forest, we saw hundreds of retreating Germans using the paths through the forest. There was little danger of our discovery by them; they were quite intent in fleeing the front lines. After a time though, there came an extended lull in the small arms fire – it seemed to get no closer – we told the commandos that, because we were starving, we had to try to make it through the lines. The lieutenant had us select branches, put them on our shoulders, and march out like an armed party. After a careful couple of hours, I welcomed the sight of the next helmet – it was that deep-dish pie-plate the Limeys wore. We'd made it! We were welcomed by the British, and offered food and drink.

A great day for us but a sad one too – April 12, 1945, the day the President died. The front line soldiers offered to share their rations with us, but we declined, and asked instead for directions to the nearest farmhouse. I walked into one nearby and told the man of the house that we wanted some meat and eggs. This old clown had a light patch on his upper lip directly under and limited by the width of his nose, from which he had just shaved a Hitler mustache. He pleaded that they were poor people, hated Nazis – particularly Hitler – and that they had no spare food. I flicked the safety off the Kraut burp-gun which I had recently acquired, and he immediately produced an egg apiece. "Nicht Genüend," – "Not enough," I said, and motioned him towards the cellar steps, following him down into the basement. It was loaded! Sausages, pork chops, vegetables – lots of glass jars full of goodies lined shelf after shelf! I had him load a large basket of these things together with eggs, eggs and more eggs! I ate three large breakfasts and vomited each, one after the other.

Further inquiry among the British relative to transportation to the rear, produced the choice to hitchhike back with empty lorries, or find the residence of the Burgomeister of the next village, and steal his automobile. We found the garage with the Mercedes, which had obviously been retired for the war years, up on blocks with a very dead battery and a very empty gas tank. Again, inquiry of the British produced a new battery and a full tank, enabling us to cruise to Brussels in some style. We sold the car in Brussels, getting enough money for a week at a hotel wine, food and a few sessions at the dog-track, before, becoming broke, we reported to the British. They put us up for a few days in comfortable quarters, issued us new British kit and sent us, by C-54, to Paris. We were weighed before the flight; I then (after two weeks fattening) weighed 135 pounds. On the flight to Paris, I was allowed the co-pilot's seat for a time. Half-way there the pilot told me to look down and there, plain as can be, were the old front line trenches from WWI!

From Paris we were taken to Camp Lucky Strike in Le Havre where, after a few days we were shipped home. In Lucky Strike the chow line was tended by Kraut POWs and, when I reached into the pot for another baked potato, a Kraut rapped my knuckles with a heavy spoon. I lost it; I wrested the spoon from him and beat him about the head until he was near unconscious. Until I was able to reflect upon this, I had been unaware of the hate that had built up in me. Much lasts."

Captain Jim Altieri. He was one of a number of Ranger enlisted men who earned hard-won battlefield commissions. (Jim Altieri collection, ASC)

BIBLIOGRAPHY

James Altieri	*Darby's Rangers: An Illustrated Portrayal of the Original Rangers* Arnold, MO Ranger Book Committee 1945
James Altieri	*The Spearheaders* Indianapolis Bobbs-Merrill 1960
William O. & Baumer, William H. Darby	*We Led the Way: Darby's Rangers* San Rafael, CA Presidio 1980
Jerome J. Haggerty	*A History of the Ranger Battalions in World War II* New York Fordham University 1982
David Hogan	*Raiders or Elite Infantry? The Changing Role of U.S. Army Rangers from Dieppe to Grenada* Westport, CT Greenwood Press 1992
Dr. Michael J. King	*William Orlando Darby: A Military Biography* No. Illinois University 1977
James Ladd	*Commandos and Rangers of World War II* New York Sterling 1989
Lucian Truscott, Jr.	*Command Missions: A Personal Story* New York Dutton 1954
David Hogan	*U.S. Army Special Operations in WWII* Washington, DC CMH 1992
Capt. Ralph Ingersoll	*The Battle is the Pay-off* New York Harcourt, Brace and Company 1943
Hartmut Schauer	*US Rangers Die Geschichte einer Elitetruppe* Stuttgart Motorbuch Verlag 1992
Terence Robertson	*Dieppe The Shame and the Glory* Boston Atlantic- Little, Brown Books 1962
Quentin Reynolds	*Raid at Dieppe* New York Random House 1943
Robert W. Black	*Rangers in World War II* New York Ivy Books 1992 *Anzio Beachhead 22 January-25 May 1944* Washington, DC CMH 1990
Lt Col. Robert Burhans	*The First Special Service Force A War History of The North Americans 1942-1944* Nashville, TN The Battery Press 1996
Anders Kjar Arnbal	*The Barrel-Land Dance Hall Rangers World War II,* June 1942-February 1944 New York Vantage Press 1993
Milton Shapiro	*Ranger Battalion: American Rangers in World War II* New York Julian Messner 1979
Dr. Michael J. King	*Leavenworth Papers No. 11 Rangers: Selected Combat Operations in World War II* Fort Leavenworth, KS Combat Studies Institute Jun-85
George Forty	*US Army Handbook 1939-1945* New York Barnes & Noble 1995
Shelby Stanton	*U.S. Army Uniforms of World War II* Mechanicsburg, PA Stackpole Books 1991
Col. Thomas H. Taylor	*Rangers Lead the Way* Paducah, Kentucky Turner Publishing Company 1996
Jean-Yves Nasse	*Green Devils! German Paratroopers 1939-1945* First Person Accounts Paris Histoire & Collections 1997
Wynford Vaughan-Thomas	*Anzio* New York Popular Library 1961
	Combined Operations: The Official Story of the Commandos New York MacMillan 1943
Donald Gilchrist	*Castle Commando* Inverness Lochaber 1960
John F. Hummer	*Infantryman's Journal* Manassas, VA Ranger Associates Inc 1981
Moen & Heinen	*Heroes Cry Too* Elk River, MN Meadowlark Publishing 2002
	The History of the American Ranger Hunter Army Air Field 1/75 Ranger Regimet, PAO 1996

COLOR PLATE COMMENTARY

A: A TYPICAL US RANGER RECRUIT IN 1942 AT ACHNACARRY, SCOTLAND, THE COMMANDO TRAINING DEPOT

1. The 1st Ranger Battalion member holds an M1 Thompson sub-machine gun with a drum magazine. He still wears the old style M1917 helmet, soon to be replaced by the new M1 steel pot.
2. 60mm M2 mortar.
2a. Mortar rounds.
3. Boys .55 antitank rifle (British); this weapon was used only in training and at Dieppe by the Rangers.
4. M-1 rifle.
5. M1919 A4 light machine gun.
6. M1911 A1 automatic pistol.
7. M1903A1 rifle w/grenade (M9 Anti-tank) on an M1 launcher.
8. M1918A2 browning automatic rifle (BAR).
9. 81mm M1 mortar.
9a. Mortar rounds.
10. Fairbairn-Sykes fighting knife; this Commando knife was issued to / bought by the 1st Ranger Battalion upon graduation.
11. Four-foot toggle rope; a series of them interlaced would make rope bridges for river crossings.
12. A Ranger is leaping off a 20-foot obstacle course in the background. Though not airborne qualified, it certainly must have seemed so to some of the recruits undergoing training. They were in the best shape of their lives.
13. Achnacarry Castle – home of the Commandos and Rangers.

B: COMMANDO AND RANGER IN OCTOBER 1942

1. A Commando and Ranger marvel at the newly created Ranger Scroll. Modern-day Ranger William D. Linn II's *History of the Ranger Scroll* explains the background to its creation:

> Fifty American Rangers of the 1st Battalion participated in the Dieppe Raid of August 1942; an unsuccessful but highly publicized first allied aggression against "Fortress Europe." American soldiers in England, attempting to capitalize on raid publicity, bragged in the pubs that they were Rangers in order to win favor with local women. Fights ensued with such frequency between Rangers and the imposters that something had to be done. Captain Roy Murray, the senior Ranger at Dieppe, recommended that Rangers be authorized their own shoulder insignia. Colonel William O. Darby requested authorization for a patch through BG Lucian Truscott and Major General Clark on

28 August, 1942 based on the following reasons:
  A. Tremendous boost to morale
  B. Soldiers all over UK are spreading stories about the recent raid and pretending to be Rangers

Once approved, October 8, 1942, Colonel Darby organized a battalion-wide contest for the best design and a prize for the winner. Sergeant Anthony Rada of HHC, a native of Flint, Michigan, won with his design of a red, white, and blue scroll patch that resembled the British commando insignia worn by the Ranger training cadre. Due to wartime shortages of blue dye, black wool became the background of the final product. The Army officially recognized the new scroll on 8 October 1942 and a supply of them were made locally in England. Though General Truscott intended them only to be worn on the service coat (dress uniform), 1st Battalion Rangers wore them proudly into battle.

In 1943, 3rd and 4th Battalions formed in Africa. Soon after the three-battalions arrived in Italy, Rangers obtained crude scrolls from local Italian sources. These examples had no uniform composition, being made of remnant cloth, wire bullion thread, and sometimes featuring irregular and reversed letters.

As American Rangers and other allied units made their way up the Italian peninsula, Axis Sally began to broadcast threats to the Rangers over Radio Berlin. Glenn Hirchert, a sniper in C Co, 1st Ranger BN recalls that every Ranger believed German policy dictated no quarter be given to Rangers who surrendered in combat. Once surrounded at Cisterna and with capture imminent, Hirchert watched Rangers draw their fighting knives and quickly remove and destroy their scrolls in hopes that they would be spared execution. The brutal German policy proved to be just effective propaganda.

2. Sergeant Anthony Rada and the famous Ranger Scroll.

3. Ranger Table of Organization June-November 1942. The battalion consisted of a headquarters company of 7 officers and 72 enlisted men (including a 10 men mess) as well as 6 line companies (A, B, C, D, E, F) of 3 officers and 59 enlisted men each. HQ Company consisted of a communications platoon and staff Platoon. Staff Platoon was divided into 3 Section: Administration & Personnel, Intel and Operations, and finally, Supply and Transportation. The Battalion Commander was Major William O. Darby, the Executive Officer and Operations and Training Officer was Captain Herman Dammer who was interestingly enough of German descent. Each line company in turn had a headquarters and two platoons. The headquarters was made of the Company Commander, a First Sergeant (Master Sergeant), a company clerk with the rank of corporal, and a private as the messenger. Each of the platoons consisted of a Platoon Headquarters, two assault sections composed of ten men and one mortar section of five men. The Platoon Headquarters totaled four men; platoon leader with the rank of Lieutenant, a platoon sergeant was a technical sergeant, a messenger and a sniper, both privates. The typical assault section of 10 rangers:

Scout (PRIVATE 1st Class)
Scout (PRIVATE 1st Class)
Section Leader Rifleman (Sergeant)
Corporal with BAR
Asst Bar, no weapon (PRIVATE 1st Class)
Rifleman (PRIVATE 1st Class)
Rifleman (PRIVATE 1st Class)
Rifleman (PRIVATE 1st Class)
Rifleman (PRIVATE 1st Class)
Rifleman (PRIVATE 1st Class)

The mortar section controlled one 60mm mortar. The Mortar Section sergeant was the gunner (staff sergeant), his assistant section sergeant was the assistant gunner (corporal) and three ammunition bearers, all privates.

The original officers of the 1st Ranger Battalion 1942:

Commanding Officer – Major William Orlando Darby
Executive Officer – Captain Herman W. Dammer
Adjutant – 2nd Lt. Howard W. Karbel
Supply Officer – 1st Lt. Axel W. Anderson
Medical Officer – 1st Lt. William A. Jarrett

Headquarters Company
Commanding Officer – 1st Lt. Gordon L. Klefman
Platoon Leader – 2nd Lt. Frederick J. Saam
Platoon Leader – 2nd Lt. George P. Sunshine

Company A
CO – Capt. Stephen J. Meade
PL – 1st Lt. Earl L. Carran
PL – 2nd Lt. Robert L. Johnson

Company B
CO – 1st Lt. Alfred H. Nelson
PL – 1st Lt. Den H. Knudson
PL – 1st Lt. Leilyn M. Young

Company C
CO – Capt. William E. Martin
PL – 1st Lt. William E. Lenning
PL – 2nd Lt. Charles M. Shunstrom

Company D
CO – Capt. Alvah M. Miller
PL – 1st Lt. Frederic F. Ahlgren
PL – 2nd Lt. William C. Davison

Company E
CO – 1st Lt. Max F. Schneider
PL – 1st Lt. Robert Flanagan
PL – 1st Lt. James B. Lyle

Company F
CO – Capt. Roy A. Murray
PL – 1st Lt. Walter F. Nye
PL – 2nd Lt. Edwin V. Loustalot

Temporary Duty (HHC, A, D, F)
PL – 1st Lt. Edward M. Olson
PL – 2nd Lt. James J. Larkin
PL – 2nd Lt. Joseph H. Randall
PL – 1st Lt. Leonard F. Dirks

There were a number of changes made to the TOE, one, for example, was to attach the mortars to company headquarters, another, the addition of a ten man mess.

C: RAID ON STATION DE SENED, NORTH AFRICA, FEBRUARY 11–14, 1943, FIGHTING ITALIAN BERSAGLIERI

Italian Bersaglieri: A corps of light infantry sharpshooters raised in 1836 by Charles Albert of Sardinia-Piedmont as part of the Sardinian Army. They served with distinction in the Crimean War and in both World Wars. The Rangers' mission was to take no prisoners except for ten men and to wreak havoc among the enemy. The First Rangers earned the nickname of "Black Death" from the Italians after conducting the night raid and killing scores in hand-to-hand combat. Ranger Sullivan describes the raid:

> 2/12/43: Friday – arrived at dawn five miles from objective, hiding out all day in cold and rain under shelterhalf – move up at 5 within 2-3 miles. Moon up. 11 P.M. on the way.
> 2/13/43: At 1 A.M. the moon went down – 100 yards from us on the plain Italians opened up with 41s and 88s. Shells bursting we attack hill. Slaughter. It's ours.
> 2/14/43: We destroyed guns with loss of one man. Killed 100-150, captured 12. Heacock hit bad. Marched full speed to outpost. Missed trucks at nite, back to Gafsa. All grumpy.

D: DARBY DESTROYING TANK, GELA, JULY 10, 1943

William "El Darbo" Darby and the rough and tough Chuck Shunstrom manning a 37mm anti-tank gun in the port city of Gela during an Italian tank counterattack. Following the assaults on Gela, the Italians and Germans threw several counterattacks at the Americans. Rangers fought with Bazookas, TNT charges and plain old guts, stopping the armored counter thrusts repeatedly. In one case, Darby and Shunstrom bumped into one of the few anti-tank guns available and engaged a "black" Renault tank. Jim Altieri recounts their deeds in *The Spearheaders*:

> Without blinking the soldier swung the jeep around, and Colonel Darby, bareheaded, sleeves rolled up, and Captain Charles Shunstrom, helmeted, bounded over and began setting up the gun for action. But before they could get it fully set up for firing, the Italian tank – bearing a death's head device – clanked around the corner and came charging down on them. Colonel Darby immediately leaped up to the jeep, swung the .30 caliber machine gun around, aimed it and splattered the ugly black turret of the tank with several withering bursts. Two cannon bursts went whishing over the heads of Darby and Shunstrom and crashed into the building behind them. Now Darby sprang from the jeep to the 37 cannon and threw in a shell, as Shunstrom peered into the sights. Darby pulled the lanyard and the shot screeched into the turret of the Italian tank as the 37 bucked back from the recoil. Again Darby threw in a shell. And again it thundered home with such accuracy and force that the Italian tank was actually flung back for several feet and then was enveloped by a sheet of searing flame. We cheered wildly. Our Ranger chief and his tough right-hand man, Captain Shunstrom, had just performed one of the war's most outstanding and selfless acts of courage and daring. That was all the Rangers needed. The rest of the tanks did not pass.

1. The 37mm Anti-tank Gun, M3
In 1935 the US Army began the development of an anti-tank gun, a newly conceived field artillery piece whose mission was to defeat the recently developed tanks of that era. It weighed less than 1,000lbs and was thus transportable by a jeep. However, the M3 37mm anti-tank gun proved too light a caliber to be effective against most tanks in the North African and European theatres of operation.

Length   10ft, 10.5in.
Width   5ft, 3.5in.
Height   3ft, 2in.
Weight   912lbs.
Firing Rate 5-20 rounds per minute
Munitions   Fixed HE (high explosive), AP (anti-personnel), Canister
Projectile Weight 1.5 to 2lbs.

2. By 1940, about 1600 French-manufactured Renault models (known as the Renault ZM) were produced. It sported a 37mm gun as well as a machine gun. The Renault became the standard French infantry tank in April 1935. Large numbers fell into German hands and had turrets removed and used for artillery tractors and ammunition carriers. A few also were converted into self-propelled artillery or antitank guns. Approximately 124 were taken over by the Italians. Radios were installed and used in Sicily.

E: RANGER, 1944

A 4th Battalion Ranger at Anzio sporting a fine moustache. The oldest profession getting along with the second oldest one.

F: RANGER, CISTERNA, JANUARY 29–30, 1944

1. Rangers surrounded near Cisterna surrender to overwhelmingly superior German forces. Germans marched captured PoWs toward the center of the Ranger perimeter. When Rangers shot German guards, PoWs in turn were bayoneted by them.
2. The M1 (left) and M9 bazookas. The IM9 version could be broken into two parts. The rocket launcher required a 2-man team, one to fire, the other to load rocket. It is 155cm in length with a maximum range of 640m, weighs 1.53kg and could penetrate armor up to 11.75cm at 90°.
3. US M3 Halftrack. Rangers needed more fire power when combating enemy tanks. The Canon Company, under the command of Capt. Charles Shunstrom, comprised four such modified vehicles with 75mm canons. They were named "Ace of Hearts," "Ace of Diamonds," "Ace of Clubs," and "Ace of Spades."
4. The Steel Pot. Boiling water or protecting the head, a GI's (Government Issue) best friend. Steel helmets were at times covered with netting or burlap to help soften the silhouette of the helmet and help camouflage.
5. Grenades. (from TM 9-1900, 1945)
5a. Fragmentation type. The Mk 2 is a typical fragmentation hand grenade. This grenade is made of cast iron varying in thickness from 1/8 to 1/4in.. The body is lemon shaped, approximately 2 1/4in. in diameter and 3 1/2in. in length without the fuse. It contains an explosive charge, which, upon detonation, breaks up the body of the grenade and fuse and projects the fragments outwards in all directions at high velocity. The body is grooved both horizontally and vertically. The fuse for this grenade has a primer, a combustible time-delay train, and a detonator. Attached to the fuse body is a safety lever held in place against the action of the striker spring by means of a safety pin. Just prior to throwing, the

safety pin is removed. When the grenade is thrown, the safety lever is pushed off by the striker, allowing the striker to impact against the primer. The primer ignites the time-delay train and after four to five seconds, this delay train causes the detonator to explode. This in turn, causes the explosive filler in the grenade to detonate, thereby fragmenting the grenade. Fragments may fly over 200 yards.

5b. Offensive type. The offensive grenade is intended to have an anti-personnel effect over a small area. It contains more explosive than the fragmentation-type grenade, approximately 1/2 pd of pressed TNT, and therefore, is more useful as a demolition agent. No fragmentation effect is obtained.

5c. and 5d. Training and Practice Hand Grenades:
This type of grenade is used in training. They may be inert (training) (5c), or loaded with a charge of black powder contained in a cloth tube (practice) (5d). In this case the charge is inserted into the filling hole, which is closed with a cork.

6a. and 6b. Chemical Hand Grenades:
Bursting type. There is only one standard chemical grenade of this type and it is known as the WP smoke grenade M15. This grenade has a drawn-steel cylindrical body similar in size to the burning type chemical hand grenades, and filled with white phosphorus. The detonating fuse used in this grenade causes it to split open and project burning particles of phosphorus over a radius of about 15 yards. This produces a dense white smoke screen and will cause casualties by burning.

6c. and 6d. Burning type. The standard container for this type of grenade is cylindrical steel can 2 3/8in. in diameter and 4 3/4in. high. The fuse for these grenades is similar to the fuse used in the Mk 2 fragmentation grenade, except that it has an igniter instead of a detonator, and has a short delay time of 2 seconds. Grenades of this type have waterproof, adhesive tape covered, smoke emission holes in the top, sides, or bottom. These grenades are described briefly as follows:

(1) CN-DM Irritant hand grenade. The products of combustion of the filler in this grenade have a harassing effect. Its principal use is in the control of civil disturbances. The burning time is 20 to 60 seconds. The filler is a composition of tear gas, vomit gas, and smokeless powder.

(2) CN tear hand grenade. This grenade is identical with the CN-DM grenade expect that it has a tear gas filler. Principal uses are in control of civil disturbances, and training in use of the gas mask.

(3) HC smoke grenade. This is an Army-Navy standard white smoke grenade, used for signaling and screening purposes. The container is standard expect that there are no emission holes in the side. The burning time is 2 to 2 1/2 minutes.

(4) TH incendiary grenade. This is an Army-navy standard munition for setting fire to enemy materiel. The container is standard expect that there are no emissions holes in the side. Clamps of steel strapping, which fit around the body of the grenade, may be used to nail the grenade against an object to be burned. The filling is termite, which burns at approximately 4,330° F for 30 to 35 seconds.

(5) Colored smoke grenade M16. This grenade, used for ground-air and ground-ground signaling purposes is made in the following colors: green, yellow, red, and violet. It is of standard construction and burns for approximately 2 minutes.

(6) Colored smoke grenade M18. This grenade, available in red, green, yellow, and violet, is also for signaling purposes. The container has emission holes in the top, and a single hole at the bottom. A tapered hole extends through the center of the grenade from the bottom emission hole to the fuse. The starter mixture lines the tapered cavity. The grenade produces a heavy smoke for approximately 1 minute.

(7) Red smoke grenade AN-M3. This grenade is an Army-Navy air forces official distress signal. It is the standard metal grenade except that the fuse lever is shortened and the body is covered with a metal jacket to which are attached three metal strips, which may be bent out from the jacket to keep the grenade from sinking into snow or soft ground. Burning time 2 to 2 1/2 minutes.

7. A Ranger sporting the popular tanker jacket during the advance on Cisterna. Two scrolls, one on each shoulder. Some Rangers who transferred from the original 1st Battalion continued to wear that scroll on the right shoulder and wore their new unit's patch on the other.

7a. During the battle for Cisterna, the Ranger Battalions encountered battle-hardened elements of the German Army, including troops from the Fallschirmjäger Lehr Regiment. Some Rangers, using farm houses or ditches for cover, fought to the bitter end. One German parachutist described their actions as heroic.

G: ROMAN COLISEUM POWS

1. Over 700 Ranger PoWs were paraded through the streets of Rome near the Coliseum. Filmed by the Germans and released in their propaganda films, some Rangers remembered Italians throwing garbage at them while others offered water and encouragement. A bitter experience no matter what.

2. Ranger officers Shunstrom and Darby

3. The scrolls of the three Ranger battalions under Colonel William Darby's command from 1943–44.

H: POW ESCAPE

Because of their training and their Ranger spirit, numerous men escaped German captivity. Some Rangers were recaptured and tried and tried again, some successfully, others not. Yet again, there were others who eluded their pursuers, joined partisans and continued the fight. A few slipped back to friendly lines. A terrific testament to the triumph of the famous Darby Ranger stanza of "onward we stagger."

Ranger Lehmann's first escape attempt ended with his recapture:

Next day, the police force of Stolpmunde, consisting of the Chief and one man, came to collect us, The Chief was a dead-ringer for Kaiser Wilhelm, the star of WWI. His snazzy, bemedaled uniform and brilliant boots were topped by a decorated Kraut helmet topped with the spearhead worn early in WWI. He even had a monocle. The fierce old man screamed at us from beginning to end of the short walk to town, the streets of which were then lined with the populace. We were "handcuffed" together with a length of chain inscribing a figure-eight about our wrists and secured with a padlock, the Chief holding his Luger to my temple.

63

INDEX

References to illustrations are shown in **bold**. Plates are shown with page and caption locators in brackets.

Achnacarry Castle, Scotland 6, 17, **A13**(33, 60)
Allen, Terry **7**
Altieri, Lt. (later Capt.) James **54**, **59**, 62
Anzio, Italy 9, **E**(36, 62), 52, **53**
Arbroath, Scotland 26
Arzew beachhead 7, **8**, **12**, **28**, 45

Barnhill (PoW) 55
Basil, Father Albert E. 25-29, **26**, **28**
beach assaults, practising **10**
Bersaglieri mountain troops 7, **C**(35, 61-62)
Bills, Sgt. Perry 52, 53

Carrickfergus, Northern Ireland 5, 6, 16
Chiunzi Pass, Italy 9, 51
Churchill, Winston 4
Cisterna, Italy 10, **F1**(38, 62), 52-54, **54**, **56**
Clarke, Lt. Col. 4
Commandos, British 4-5, 15, **54**
  No. 4: **6**, 6
Conca-Cisterna road **55**

Dammer, Capt. (later Maj.) Herman W. 7, 9, 17-18, 61
Dammer Force 7
Darby, Capt. (later Brig-Gen.) William Orlando (El Darbo) **5**, 5-6, **7**, 7, 9, 10, 17-18, **18**, 24, 26, 29
  destroying tank at Gela **D1**(36, 62)
  as PoW **G2**(39, 63)
Darby Ranger Force **5**, 9, 10
"Death Slide" **24**
Dieppe raid **6**, 6-7, 42-45, **43**, **44**
Dirks, 1st Lt. Leonard F. 42-45
Dobson, Maj. John 10
Dundee, Scotland 22

El Guettar, battle of **9**, 9, **11**, 27, 47
enemy troops 32, 41 *see also* German troops
enlistment 14-15
equipment 30-31 *see also* helmets; jacket, tanker
Evans, Ranger (later 2nd Lt.) Warren 17-18, 32, 41
  Sened Station raid 45-47
  Italy 50-51

Fairszien 55-56
food rations **29**, 32
Fredericks, Ranger Don 32

Gela, Italy **D1**(36, 62), 49-50, **50**
German troops **F7a**(38, 63), **42** *see also* enemy troops

halftracks **F1**, **F3**(38, 62)
Hall, Ranger PFC Edward J. **55**
Hardenberg (PoW) 55
Hartle, Gen. Russell P. 5
helmets **F4**(38, 62)
Hirchert, Glenn 61
Hodel, Ranger 53, 54

Hurst, Larry 53, 54
hygiene, personal **31**, 32, **41**

Ingram, Sgt. John **8**
Italian Bersaglieri mountain troops 7, **C**(35, 61-62)
Italians 41
Italy 9-10, 50-51 *see also* Cisterna; Conca-Cisterna road; Gela; Rome; Sicily

jacket, tanker **F7**(38, 62)
Jackson (PoW) 55
Johnson (PoW) 57-58

Kiernan (PoW) 57-58

latrines 32
Lavin, Capt. James **53**
Laycock, Brig. 26
Lehmann, Ranger Carl 4-5, 25, 29
  as PoW 54-59
    recaptured **H**(40, 63)
  Cisterna 52-54
Licata, Italy 49-50
Linn, Ranger William D., II 60-61
Lowell, PFC (later 1st Sgt.) Robert **8**

Marshall, Gen. George 5
McCaughan, Sgt. Maj. 20, 21
McClaren, Misses 23
McMahon, John 55
Meade, Capt. Stephen J. **17**, 21
Mercuriali, Ranger Gino 32
Miller, Maj. Alvah M. 10, 52
Munro, Scotty 53
Murray, Capt. (later Maj.) Roy A. 9, 42, 60

New York, USS 15
North Africa **27**, **48** *see also* Arzew beachhead; El Guettar, battle of; Operation Torch
Nunnelly, Capt. George C. **53**

officers, 1st Ranger Battalion 61
Operation Torch 7, **13**, **25**, 45
organization table **B3**(34, 61)

Patton, Gen. George 27
police chief, German **H**(40, 63)
prison camp, Rummelsberg (Stalag II B) 54-55, 57
prisoners-of-war
  Afrika Korps **50**
  Ranger **G1**(39, 63), 54-59
    escapes **H**(40, 63), 56, 57-59 *see also* "Ranger Houdini Club"
  Vichy French soldiers **27**

Queen Elizabeth 24

Rada, Ranger Sgt. Anthony 7, **B2**(34, 61), **41**
Ranger Force, 6615: 9
"Ranger Houdini Club" 10
Ranger Scrolls 7, **B**(34, 60-61), **G3**(39, 63)
Rangers, US **4**, **6**
Reed, Lt. Rip 53

Rice, Sarah 23
Rome, Italy **G1**(39, 63)
Rommel, General Erwin 32, **41**
Roosevelt, President Franklin D. 5
Royal Scotsman 23
Royal Ulsterman 23
Ruona (PoW) 57-58

Sapsara, Paul 55
Sened Station, Tunisia, raid 7, **C**(35, 61-62), 45-47
Shunstrom, Captain Charles M. "Chuck" **D1**(36, 62), **G2**(39, 63), **57**
Sicily 49-50, **50**, **51**, **52**
Space, Bill 55
Stern, Phil **11**, **16**, **41**
Stolpmunde **H**(40, 63)
Stroud, Corp. Pressley P. **54**
Sullivan, Audrey **14**
Sullivan, Ranger PFC (later Sgt.) Thomas S. "Sully" **14**, 14-15, 16-17
  North Africa 45, **47**, 47-48
  Sened Station 62
  Sicily 49-50, 51, **53**
  training 20-22, 23-24
Szima, Ranger Alex **44**

tank, Renault **D2**(36, 62)
tank destroyer, German **54**
training 17, **19**, 19-22, **22**, 23-24, **24**, **A12**(33, 60), 42-43, **43**, 45
Truscott, Col. (later Gen.) Lucian K., Jr. 5, 61

Ulster Monarch 23
United States Army
  1st Infantry Division 7
  1st Ranger Battalion 5-6, 9-10, 17, 22, **C**(35, 61-62), **45**, 52, 61
    Company A 7, 45-47, **47**, 48, 61
    Company B 7, 48, 61
    Company C 7, 48, 61
    Company D 7, 24, 48, 61
    Company E 7, 46, 48, 61
    Company F 7, 46, 48, 61
    Company G 7, 61
  3rd Ranger Battalion 9-10, 48, 52, **53**
  4th Ranger Battalion 9, 10, **E**(37, 62), 48, **53**, 55
  34th Division, 168th Regiment **14**, 14

Vaughan, Lt. Col. Charles **18**, 18-19
volunteering 15-17

Weakes (PoW) 57-58
weapons 29, **A1-A11**(33, 60)
  anti-tank gun, M3 37 mm **D1**(36, 62)
  bazookas, M1/M9 **F2**(38, 62)
  grenades **F5**, **F6**(38, 62-63)
    No. 74 "Sticky" 29
  knife, Fairbairn-Sykes **12**, **A10**(33, 60)
  pistol, .45-cal M1911A1 automatic 29, **A6**(33, 60)
  rifles, .30-cal M1903/M1903A1 magazine 29, **A7**(33, 60)
  sub-machine guns, .45-cal M1/M1A1 Thompson 29, **A1**(33, 60)

64